$\mathcal{A}$CKNOWLEDGMENTS

THIS BOOK REPRESENTS THE CONTRIBUTIONS OF THE teachers, mentors, and colleagues who have made family history easy... and ever so enjoyable for me. Because I couldn't phrase concepts better than they have, no less than fifty of these authorities are quoted in their respective areas of expertise. I am grateful to them all.

I particularly want to thank my good friend Sandra Luebking, FUGA, for influencing, advising, and contributing generously to every phase of this work; my husband, Bob, for putting up with yet another project of mine; daughters Diana Sullivan and Tricia Stitz for never-ending support and encouragement; daughter, Juliana Smith, for contributing the very important chapter on computer use; daughter, Laura Pfeiffer for patiently working out the project details and offering so many helpful suggestions; John P. Sullivan for designing the cover; Ryan Van Fleet for providing professional and finishing touches on the cover; Matt Grove for his editorial skills, and helpful guidance; Roger Joslyn, CG, FUGA, FASG, for peer reviewing and making helpful suggestions; John Tolman for cheering me on and convincing me of the need for this book; André Brummer for his encouragement and for shepherding the book to completion; Catherine Horman for her cheerful patience with me while proofing and checking details; Jennifer Utley for her wisdom and great skills in turning a plain manuscript into the book I had hoped for; and Paul Allen and Dan Taggart for making the book possible.

FAMILY HISTORY
Made Easy

FAMILY HISTORY
Made Easy

Loretto Dennis Szucs

Library of Congress Cataloging-in-Publication Data

Szucs, Loretto Dennis.
Family history made easy / by Loretto Dennis Szucs.
p. cm.
Includes bibliographical references and index.
ISBN 0-916489-72-8 (alk. paper)
1. United States—Genealogy—Handbooks, manuals, etc. 2. Genealogy.
I. Title.
CS16.S98   1998
929'.1'072073--dc21   98-15460

© 1998 Ancestry Incorporated
P.O. Box 476
Salt Lake City, Utah 84110-0476

First printing 1998
10 9 8 7 6 5 4 3 2 1

Printed in the United States of America

CONTENTS

*I*NTRODUCTION

Human beings look separate because you see them walking about separately. But then we are so made that we can see only the present moment. If we could see the past, then of course it would look different. For there was a time when every man was part of his mother, and (earlier still) part of his father as well, and when they were part of his grand parents. If you could see humanity spread out in time, as God sees it, it would look like one single growing thing—rather like a very complicated tree. Every individual would appear connected with every other.

C. S. LEWIS

*W*HO WERE YOUR ANCESTORS? WHERE DID THEY live? What choices made by these men and women over the generations have influenced the way you live and think? In many ways, the ancestors we can never meet have affected our lives and molded our destinies. Although we are not clones of our ancestors, their blood runs in our veins, and we have inherited pieces of their genetic makeup. Their physical traits, values, and attitudes have been transmitted from generation to generation, showing up in the way we look, think, and

act. Our ancestors amount to more than just a string of lifeless names on a chart. They made a difference in our world. They still do. But it is strange how little most of us know about them or the times in which they lived.

For most of us, nothing has more power to attract or hold the imagination than the thought of who we are and where we came from. Alex Haley, the author of *Roots*, observed that "in all of us there is a hunger, marrow deep, to know our heritage—to know who we are and where we have come from." Yet for many, these questions seem unanswerable.

Busy and ever-changing lifestyles have caused many people to lose sight of their family origins. From earliest times, American families have been continually on the move. Most of our ancestors were uprooted from their home countries, moved from seaboard states to inland frontiers, from farms to cities, from neighborhoods to suburbs—always upward in status when they could. With so much mobility, families have been scattered and lines of communication broken, and many of our ancestors' stories and traditions have vanished in the process.

But the past has not been totally obliterated. Wonderful records that hold secrets to your family's past have been and are being preserved and made more accessible. A tremendous surge of interest in family history in recent years has dramatically improved the potential for finding and using information about our ancestors. Genealogy, once the avocation of an elite few, has rapidly grown into a serious yet enjoyable diversion for millions of Americans from all backgrounds. In keeping with contemporary thought that history is not created by the famous alone, more and more students from grade school to college are being encouraged to investigate their ancestry. Most individuals, however, are attracted to family history because they have discovered the thrill that comes from personal involvement and the real detective work required in every stage of research.

FAMILY HISTORY IS GAINING IN POPULARITY

Obviously, the interest in genealogy is not a recent phenomenon. In one form or another it has been with humanity since the beginnings of civilization, as shown by the fact that many creation myths have a genealogical component or epilogue, explaining the origins and structure of human society as well as the cosmos.

> *In medieval and early modern Europe the recording and perpetuation of genealogy was largely limited to elites, if for no other reason than that literacy outside the church was largely confined to these classes or to the service of these classes. But by the late eighteenth century people without title were recording family data in their Bibles with the obvious intention of passing the information on to succeeding generations.*
>
> DAVID T. THACKERY,
> Curator, Local and Family History,
> The Newberry Library, Chicago
> "Tracking African American Family History"
> *The Source: A Guidebook of American Genealogy*

- In a recent national poll, 74.4 percent of the respondents indicated that they are extremely or very interested in learning more about their family tree (*USA Today*).

- "...genealogy has gone from spectator sport to major league passion. ...42 million Americans have started to trace their heritage" (*Newsweek*, February 24, 1997).

- Seventy-two million Americans are somewhat interested in genealogy (Maritz Marketing Research in American Demographics).

As interest has grown, demand and technological advances have brought previously unavailable sources of information practically to our doorsteps. Whether the search for information stems from simple curiosity or a compelling need to know what hereditary traits run in the family, there are ever-increasing ways to find answers.

Family history research combines elements of a great detective mystery and an enormous jigsaw puzzle. You'll experience the thrill of finding a particularly elusive individual—then satisfaction as you add his or her name to your family's story.

There is no specific formula that can be used to trace any family history. Every family is unique, having a different assortment of people who lived in different places under different circumstances. While a book of this limited size cannot provide detailed information on all sources available to family historians, *Family History Made Easy* covers the basic tools and provides essential instructions. My intention is to suggest some of the easiest ways to find, document, and preserve your family history. A list of recommended reading and some useful addresses are also included.

If you are just beginning to look into your family's history, you may wonder about the difference between the terms genealogy and family history. Genealogy is essentially the charting of lineal descent (that is, the direct line of descent—parents, grandparents, great-grandparents, etc.), either male or female. Family history research, on the other hand, adds color by including historical and biographical details to what are otherwise lackluster lists of names, dates, and relationships. There will always be those who are interested only in collecting the greatest numbers of names and dates. While this book may be helpful if that is your plan, I hope it will encourage you to do more. *Family History Made Easy* is designed to entice you to jump in with both feet and feel the excitement of discovery. Delving into your family history can be one of the most intellectually stimulating, absorbing, and satisfying ways you will ever find to spend your time. This guide is an introduction to the wide and rich variety of materials that you can use to build a bridge for your personal journey back in time.

BEGINNING YOUR FAMILY HISTORY

These are exciting times that we live in! With technology advancing exponentially every couple of moments, it seems, and with more and more individuals coming into the field of genealogy, we have a convergence of some really wonderful things—a lot of talent, a lot of possibilities, and the technology to help us manage those opportunities.

CURT WITCHER, MLS, FUGA
Manager, Historical Genealogical Department,
Allen County Public Library
Coordinator of the Civil War Soldiers Names Input Project
Columnist, *Ancestry* magazine

It's true. We are ever so fortunate to live in this age of technology, where we have so much available to us so quickly. It is a natural instinct to want to learn about those who lived long before us. But most of us bemoan the fact that our ancestors left no paper trail for us to follow—not even a clue to help begin a family history project. So, before you get started, think of those who will come after you; in your eagerness to go back in time, don't forget to leave a record of your own life so that those who come after will not have the same problems. Chapter 12, "Preserving the Past for the Future: Organizing Your Family History," offers some suggestions that will add more fun to your project. Document (prove), as much as possible, what you state about yourself. Proof may be found in the form of a birth certificate, religious records, school records, degrees, licenses, military records, marriage records, ownership records, membership records, photographs, etc. See more about potential sources used by family historians on page 187.

Work backward, one generation at a time. Gather as much information as possible about your parents, grandparents, and so on. A good genealogy or family history never assumes anything. Each name, date, and place should be documented—proved by reference to the same types of records mentioned above. And remember, while it may be very tempting to skip a generation or more in order make a connection to some famous family or character in history, that approach can easily land you in the wrong family tree!

COUSIN FINDER INSTRUCTIONS: To determine a relationship between two people, enter the common ancestor for both people in block 1. Next, enter that common ancestor's descendants in the numbered blocks until you've entered the two people for whom you wish to determine a relationship (one family line along the top and the other down the side). Follow the column and row for the two people into the table. The intersecting block shows the relationship.

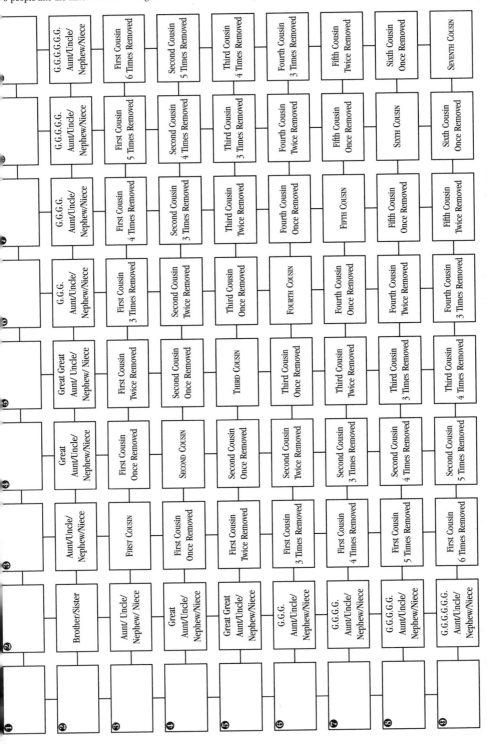

Chapter One

$\mathcal{F}$AMILY $\mathcal{H}$OME SOURCES

Home sources offer three significant opportunities to a family historian. First, the very fact of their survival can tell much about the caretaker—the person or persons who found them to be worthy of saving. Second, they can be genuine sources of evidence: the will preserved for generations that names all of a great-grandfather's children (even the illegitimate ones) or the record of an infant's baptism. Third, a home source can be a key that unlocks the approach to an official record, such as a vital record, a cemetery record, or a court case to name a few possibilities.

SANDRA HARGREAVES LUEBKING, FUGA
Editor, Federation of Genealogical Societies Forum
In *The Source: A Guidebook of American Genealogy*

SEARCH FOR ITEMS IN YOUR OWN HOME

Your own home is a likely source of information regarding previous generations. Almost every family cherishes remem-

1

brances of its past generations in some form or another: Bibles, diaries, journals, scrapbooks, letters, and other sentimental items are obvious sources of information. And there may well be other, less

obvious, sources in your home: certificates, newspaper clippings, school records, military records, and many other items can offer important clues and documentation.

You're looking for names and dates and also for clues that can lead you to other records; for example, an old letter might mention that an ancestor arrived in the United States on a certain date at a particular port. Using this information, you could search for the ancestor's name in passenger arrival lists (discussed in chapter 3, "Federal Records"); such a list might then indicate where the person lived before emigrating. Record the information you find and note the source of any genealogically or historically useful information you find in your immediate surroundings.

Brooklyn, N. Y., May 31ᵉʳ 1890

M̲o̲

OFFICES
AND
STORES FITTED UP.
Jobbing
PROMPTLY ATTENDED TO.

To R. F. DYER, Dᵉ

CARPENTER & BUILDER,

237 STATE STREET,

BET. SMITH ST., AND BOERUM PLACE.

This is my 21ᵉʳ Birthday as you can see that I'm in Business for myself, doing pretty good. I got a Horse + wagon, a nice office, shop + yard. I got one man working for me + I pay him $2.50 a day — 8 hours. he is a good workman. I expect to put on one more man soon.

LEARN WHAT YOUR LIVING RELATIVES KNOW

The next step is to question relatives who may have helpful facts, artifacts, or documents. If you are fortunate enough to have older members in the family, approach them first. It is wise to take good notes or, better still, to make audio or video

recordings of an interview. Time has a way of fogging memories, and a "fact" presented with the best of intentions may be inaccurate. Unfortunately, too, we all interpret information in our own way and tend to "twist" it in the retelling, so keep this in mind as you analyze and record information.

Almost every family has intriguing traditions and beliefs that have been passed down through the generations. Older family members will recall the family's weaknesses and its strengths, its happiest and saddest days—but will be selective in disclosing anything negative. Most of us have heard stories of illustrious ancestors, and if you are lucky, you will be able to verify (document) these nuggets. Unfortunately, many family stories are just that— stories!

All stories are worth preserving—as long as you cite the source of the information and do not accept it or incorporate into the family history without first proving it. As some say, just because Santa Claus is a myth doesn't mean that we have to take him out and shoot him. Frequently it is these fascinating tales that draw us into family history to start with. Sometimes you will find that hidden in a lot of fiction is at least a touch of truth. That "touch" may be the key to making a connection that you can really prove. To ensure getting off on the right foot in gathering information and keeping records straight, consult Elizabeth Shown Mills's *Evidence! Citation and Analysis for the Family Historian.*

Distant relatives—those who are geographically distant and those who are not closely related—may also have critical or helpful answers to some of your questions. It is always possible that someone in another branch of the family or in a distant location has inherited a document or a memory you need to piece things together. After you have spoken with all of your nearby and immediate relatives, don't overlook more-distant relatives. (If you interview someone over the telephone, be especially careful about taking accurate notes, and copy them over immediately after the call while your memory is still fresh.)

Finding long-lost cousins may not be as difficult as you might think. With an online directory search via the Internet you can look up anyone with a listed telephone number in the United States; Switchboard at http://www.switchboard.com is one online directory. (If you don't have Internet access from your home, most public libraries offer Internet access and have telephone directories on CD-ROM. More fascinating potential for Internet research is discussed in chapter 10, "Family History, Computers, and the Internet.")

If you are writing a letter soliciting information, there are several important things to keep in mind. It is a common courtesy, especially when you are asking for something, to send a self addressed, stamped envelope (commonly referred to as an SASE). Your chances of getting a reply are much greater with this approach. And make every effort to keep the letter neat and brief! Long, wordy letters tend to over-

whelm people and to be pushed aside. A warm, courteous, and short letter that teases a memory about names, places, and events is best.

Home sources, including letters and interviews with relatives, are probably the most tantalizing of sources. It is usually from personal belongings and eyewitness accounts of living family members that we can best catch the spirit and character of the family. Cherished stories, photographs, and mementos breathe life into otherwise boring statistics. It is these heirlooms and traditions that have the power to inspire us. It is these warm and human dimensions of research that make us want to preserve our findings for the generations to come.

As you find each new piece of information, you'll find yourself anticipating the next find that will lead further back in time. And when you are discouraged because you've run out of ways to continue your research, you can always go back to your home sources for inspiration. You'll also find it helpful to return to home sources for another reason: something that you overlooked in a document or photograph when you first saw it can have a new significance after you've accumulated more information and knowledge on the subject.

SELECTED READING

Mills, Elizabeth Shown. *Evidence! Citation and Analysis for the Family Historian.* Baltimore: Genealogical Publishing Co., 1997.

Szucs, Loretto Dennis, and Sandra Hargreaves Luebking, eds. *The Source: A Guidebook of American Genealogy.* Rev. ed. Salt Lake City: Ancestry, 1997.

Chapter Two

$\mathcal{P}$UBLISHED $\mathcal{S}$OURCES
AND $\mathcal{L}$IBRARIES

Library sources are essential in the ever-expanding field of genealogy. For beginners who are just starting to research their family history and for more advanced researchers who believe they have exhausted potential sources of information, local libraries offer many sources that await discovery, and much information is hidden in basic reference sources.

MARTHA L. HENDERSON
Genealogy Librarian and Department Head,
Mid-Continent Public Library System, Independence, Missouri
"General Reference"
In *Printed Sources: A Guide to Published Genealogical Records*

$\mathcal{A}$FTER YOU HAVE COLLECTED INFORMATION FROM FAMILY members and exhausted home sources, libraries are often the best places to explore next. Even the smallest public libraries generally have reference sections that include major directories, indexes, and reference materials that will open new doors.

Libraries in the places where your ancestors once lived may have special collections of materials that can't be found anywhere else. Local libraries usually have historical works that pertain to the immediate area and biographical sources for prominent citizens. Local histories make fascinating reading; you may find a county or town history that will give you a close look at the places and times your ancestors lived in. These books may even name your ancestors and provide biographical sketches and portraits. Often the local library will contain bound records, newspapers, school yearbooks, and other information sources. Some libraries maintain scrapbooks, photograph collections, and obituary files. Some even have large collections of genealogy and family history books, microfilm, microfiche, CD-ROMs, and other computerized sources.

State libraries, college and university libraries, and many private libraries also house treasures for family historians. In the introduction to *Printed Sources: A Guide to Published Genealogical Records*, Kory Meyerink states:

> The *American Library Directory*...lists more than thirty-five thousand public, academic, government, and special libraries in the United States and Canada. Within each state or province, cities are listed alphabetically; each library is listed under the city where it is located. Information given includes the name, address, telephone number, and a brief description of the library, such as the size of its collection, any special collections it has, and its publications and other interests.

SPECIAL GUIDES

> *The location and correct identification of records is the under-pinning of all we do in genealogical research, and if we are careful at this early stage, the rest of our genealogical work will benefit.*
>
> ROBERT CHARLES ANDERSON, CG, FASG
> Director, New England Historic Genealogical
> Society's Great Migration Study Project
> In *The Source: A Guidebook of American Genealogy*

Finding the records that will lead you closer to your ancestor is usually the hardest part of any search. A wonderful array of guides have been published to help you with specific research areas, and more are being published in book and electronic form. Among them are ethnic guides and guides to research in foreign countries. There are also guides to specific types of records and guides designed to help you research in particular places in the United States. These instructional works can suggest unique sources, and they will probably save you significant time and effort.

In *Printed Sources: A Guide to Published Genealogical Records*, editor and author Kory Meyerink and a variety of genealogical experts bring to light a great many research prizes that exist in the form of published records—original records reproduced as transcripts or abstracts and various other published works. The book explains why the published records were created, how to find them, and how to best use them for your family history research challenges. *Printed Sources'* topics include instructional materials; maps, atlases, and gazetteers; bibliographies and catalogs; censuses;

family histories and genealogies; and other types of published sources.

If your research questions concern American sources, there are some important guides that will ease you through the maze of genealogically and biographically important materials created and stored by bureaucracies large and small across the United States. *The Source: A Guidebook of American Genealogy* is a standard reference in the field. As Robert Charles Anderson notes in its introduction:

> The purpose of *The Source* is to indicate to you what sorts of records are available to family historians and how to find them. In the course of reviewing this material, you, the researcher, will find much information that will assist you in the careful documentation of these records, as well as some guideposts toward the first steps in analyzing the documents.

With detailed maps by renowned mapmaker William Dollarhide and descriptions of sources available for every state and county in the United States, *Ancestry's Red Book: American State, County, and Town Sources* can serve as an important tool. *Ancestry's Red Book* provides a short history for every state, along with directions for researching special census records, background sources, guides, and maps; vital, land, court, tax, probate, cemetery, military, immigration, ethnic, and church records; newspaper collections; and other collections unique to each state. In the section on New York, for example, Roger Joslyn notes that:

> *The New York Genealogical and Biographical Record* is the oldest continuing genealogical periodical in the state. Published since 1870, it is the quarterly of the New York Genealogical and Biographical Society and has printed numerous source records, compiled genealogies, and other fine articles concerning New York history and genealogy.

LOCAL GUIDES

A number of genealogical and historical guides for specific cities have been published over the past few years, and more are in the development stages. An example is Estelle Guzik, ed., *Genealogical Resources in the New York Metropolitan Area.* Though published by the Jewish Genealogical Society, this volume is not limited to Jewish sources. The majority of the facilities covered are in New York City, but six suburban counties in New York state and New Jersey are also included.

For Chicago, springboard for the westward migration and home to millions, there is a

special guide that covers virtually every genealogical and historical source from architectural history sources to vital records. *Chicago and Cook County: A Guide to Research* provides addresses and telephone numbers for the repositories of hundreds of record locations and discusses how to use the records. It also offers tips for reconstructing stories and documents lost in the Great Chicago Fire of 1871.

Robert W. Barnes's *Guide to Research in Baltimore City and County* provides important details about genealogical information in archives, libraries, repositories, maps, biographical sources, cemeteries, ethnic histories, newspapers, occupational and political sources, and some hard-to-find city records.

Look for more of these city-specific guides to appear in the near future. Some important guides to state collections are described in chapter 5.

FAMILY HISTORIES

> *Do we really write for our own family? If that is so, then I think it is absolutely amazing...the number of books written by genealogists who are just writing for their own*

family...that end up on library shelves. There they are not only being used by other genealogists, but also by the new breed of historian, cultural geographer, demographer, or medical researcher, who recognizes the potential genealogy has to offer to the academic world.

ELIZABETH SHOWN MILLS, CG, CGL, FASG
Editor, *NGS Quarterly*

Thousands of family histories have been published since the 1800s. It may be that some near or distant relative of yours has already researched and published a history about one or more of your family lines. But any published source must be used with caution. Some of these homespun publications have not been well researched or documented, and some contain more misinformation than truth.

Not every library, of course, will have all of the works mentioned here, but even the smallest libraries are likely to have some of the most important genealogy and family history reference works on their shelves. Just a glance at some of the better volumes will provide an amazing overview of records that may divulge fascinating details about your family.

As you search for genealogies or histories that help overcome gaps in records, remember that your local libraries will likely be connected to one or more of several nationwide computer library networks. These networks permit librarians to search for copies of books available through interlibrary loan. Talk to librarians about how they can borrow books that are available in faraway libraries. Even books you find in the collections of the Library of Congress—which does not loan books—may be available at a public or college library elsewhere in the United States.

RAYMOND S. WRIGHT III, PH.D.
Brigham Young University
Columnist for *Ancestry* magazine

SELECTED READING

Barnes, Robert W. *Guide to Research in Baltimore City and County.* Westminster, Md.: Family Line Publications, 1989.

Eichholz, Alice, ed. *Ancestry's Red Book: American State, County and Town Sources.* Rev. ed. Salt Lake City: Ancestry, 1992.

Guzik, Estelle, ed. *Genealogical Resources in the New York Metropolitan Area.* New York: Jewish Genealogical Society, 1989.

Hogan, Roseann Reinemuth. *Kentucky Ancestry: A Guide to Genealogical and Historical Research.* Salt Lake City: Ancestry, 1992.

Meyerink, Kory. M., ed. *Printed Sources: A Guide to Published Genealogical Records.* Salt Lake City: Ancestry, 1998.

Mills, Elizabeth Shown. *Evidence! Citation and Analysis for the Family Historian.* Baltimore: Genealogical Publishing Co., 1997.

Szucs, Loretto Dennis. *Chicago and Cook County: A Guide to Research.* Salt Lake City: Ancestry, 1996.

Szucs, Loretto Dennis, and Sandra Hargreaves Luebking, eds. *The Source: A Guidebook of American Genealogy.* Rev. ed. Salt Lake City: Ancestry, 1997.

Chapter Three

ℱEDERAL ℛECORDS

The public, when viewing the National Archives, usually associates it with the great documents of American history— the Declaration of Independence, the Constitution and the Bill of Rights, Lincoln's Emancipation Proclamation, and the Louisiana Purchase Treaty. That view is not incorrect for these archival treasures are all there. But the National Archives is much more, for under its care are hundreds of millions of items which literally document the lives of every American from the most famous to the ordinary.

ROBERT M. WARNER,
Archivist of the United States, 1980–85
In *The Archives: A Guide to the National Archives Field Branches*

𝒯HE VARIOUS RECORDS THAT HAVE BEEN CREATED BY the federal government comprise a valuable source of information. While federal records were not created for family historians or with family historians in mind, some government records are rich in historical and biographical information. In some instances federal records, many of which are widely accessible, will be the starting point for discovering your family's history. Most census, military, immigration, and land records used regularly by family historians are held by the National Archives and Records Administration (NARA) in Washington, D.C., and its regional archives.

CENSUS RECORDS

> *There are numerous ways to determine the location in which to concentrate research for an ancestor. One of the most popular and productive is the census.*
>
> ALICE EICHHOLZ, PH.D.
> In Ancestry's *Red Book: American State, County and Town Sources*

Since 1790, the U.S. government has taken a nationwide population count every ten years. Unique in scope and often surprisingly detailed, the census population schedules created from 1790 to 1920 are among the most used of records created by the federal government. Over the course of two centuries the United States has changed significantly, and so has the census. From the six basic questions asked in the 1790 census, the scope and categories of information have changed and expanded dramatically.

Early censuses were essentially basic counts of inhabitants; but as the nation grew, so did the need for statistics that would reflect the characteristics of the people. In 1850, the focus of the census was radically broadened. Going far beyond the vague questions previously asked of heads of households, the 1850 census enumerators were instructed to ask the age, sex, color, occupation, birthplace, and other questions regarding every individual in every household. Succeeding enumerations solicited more information; by 1920, census enumerators asked twenty-nine questions of every head of household and almost as many questions of everyone else in the residence. (Only a very small segment of the 1890 census remains; a fire in the

Commerce Department destroyed the vast majority of the original records for that year. Because of privacy considerations, census records less than seventy-two years old are not available to the general public; thus, the 1920 census is the most recent available to the public.)

Few, if any, records reveal as many details about individuals and families as do the U.S. federal censuses. The population schedules are successive "snapshots" of Americans that depict where and how they were living at particular periods in the past. Once home sources and library sources have been exhausted, the census is often the best starting point for further genealogical research. Statewide indexes (see "Indexes," below) are available for almost every census; they are logical tools for locating individuals whose precise place of residence is unknown. While some inaccuracies are to be expected in census records, they still provide some of the most fascinating and useful pieces of personal history to be found in any source. If nothing else, census records are important sources for placing individuals in specific places at specific times. Additionally, information found in the census will often point to other sources critical to complete research, such as court, land, military, immigration, naturalization, and vital records.

The importance of census records does not diminish over time in any research project. It is always wise to return to these records as discoveries are made in other sources because, as you discover new evidence about individuals, some information that seemed unrelated or unimportant in a first look at the census may take on new importance.

When you can't find family, vital, or religious records, census records may be the only means of documenting the events of a person's life. Vital registration—the official recording of births, deaths, and marriages—did not begin until around 1920 in many areas of the United States, and fires, floods and other disasters since have destroyed some official government records. When other documentation is missing, census records are frequently used by individuals who must prove their age or citizenship status (or that of their parents) for Social Security benefits, insurance, passports, and other important reasons.

HOW TO FIND CENSUS RECORDS

All available federal census schedules (those made from 1790 to 1920) have been microfilmed and are available at the National Archives in Washington, D.C.; at the National Archives' regional archives; at the Family History Library of The Church of Jesus Christ of Latter-day Saints (LDS church) in Salt Lake City and LDS family history centers throughout North America (see chapter 8, "The Family History Library and Its Centers"); at many large libraries; in genealogical society libraries; and through companies that lend microfilmed records. Some state and local agencies have census schedules for the state or area they serve. Generally, microfilm copies may be borrowed through interlibrary loan.

STARTING WITH THE CENSUS

It is usually best to begin a census search in the most recently available census records (1920) and to work from what is already known about a family. With any luck, birthplaces and other clues found in these more recent records will point to locations of earlier residence.

ARRANGEMENT OF CENSUS RECORDS

Census schedules are arranged by census year and thereunder alphabetically by state, then (generally) alphabetically by county. To begin a search, you must know the state in which the subject of your interest lived during the census taking, and you may need to know the county and at least an approximate address if the name is a common one.

For early censuses or for schedules from sparsely populated areas, one roll of microfilm may contain all the schedules for one county or several small counties; but in heavily populated areas, there may be many rolls for a single county. The arrangement of surnames on a page of the schedule is usually in the order in which the enumerator visited the households. To search for a particular name in the schedules may necessitate scanning every page of a district; however, the increasingly numerous indexes to federal censuses and other finding aids have dramatically reduced such tedious work.

INDEXES

Federal census indexes exist for every state up to and including the 1850 census; the schedules for many states have been indexed up to and including 1870, and a few have been completed for 1880. Indexes may be in book, microfilm, computer diskette, or CD-ROM form. There are microfilmed indexes or partial indexes for the 1880, 1900, 1910, and 1920 censuses. Archives and libraries that have copies of the census schedules on microfilm usually have indexes to complement their collections.

THE SOUNDEX INDEX SYSTEM

An index and filing system called the Soundex is the key to finding the names of individuals among the millions listed in the 1880, 1900, 1910, and 1920 federal censuses. The Soundex indexes include heads of households and persons of different surnames in each household.

The Soundex indexes are coded surname (last name) indexes based on the progression of consonants rather than the spelling of the surname. This coding system was developed and implemented by the Work Projects Administration (WPA) in the 1930s for the Social Security Administration in response to that agency's need to identify individuals who would be eligible to apply for old-age benefits. Because early birth records are unavailable in a number of states, the 1880 census manuscripts became the most dependable means of verifying dates of birth for people who would qualify—those born in the 1870s. Widespread misspelling caused so many problems in matching names, however, that the Soundex system was adopted. Because locating eligible Social Security beneficiaries was the sole reason for creating the 1880 Soundex, only households with children ten years of age or under were included in that index. All households were included in the Soundex indexes for the 1900, 1910, and 1920 censuses.

How the Soundex Works

Soundex index entries are arranged on cards, first in Soundex code order and then alphabetically by first name of the head of household. For each person in the house, the Soundex card should show name, race, month and year of birth, age, citizenship status, place of residence by state and county, civil division, and, where appropriate for urban dwellers, the city name, house number, and street name. The cards also list the volume number, enumeration district number, and page and line numbers of the original schedules from which the information was taken.

Coding a Surname

To search for a name it is necessary to first determine its Soundex code. Every Soundex code consists of a letter and three numbers; for example, S655. The letter is always the first letter of the surname. The numbers are assigned according to the Soundex coding guide below.

Code key letters and equivalents:

1   B, P, F, V
2   C, S, K, G, J, Q, X, Z
3   D, T
4   L
5   M, N
6   R

The letters *A*, *E*, *I*, *O*, *U*, *W*, *Y*, and *H* are disregarded. Consonants in each surname which sound alike have the same code.

Use of Zero in Coding Surnames

A surname that yields no code numbers, such as Lee, is L000; one yielding only one code number, such as Kuhne, takes two zeros and is coded as K500; and one yielding two code numbers takes just one zero; thus, Ebell is coded as E140. No more than three digits are ever used, so Ebelson would be coded as E142, not E1425.

Names With Prefixes

Because the Soundex does not treat prefixes consistently, surnames beginning with, for example, Van, Vander, Von, De, Di, or Le may be listed with or without the prefix, making it necessary to search for both possibilities. Search for the surname vanDevanter, for example, with and without the "van-" prefix. Mc- and Mac- are not considered prefixes.

Names With Adjacent Letters
Having the Same Equivalent Number

When two key letters or equivalents appear together or one key letter immediately follows or precedes an equivalent, the two are coded as one letter with a single number. (Surnames may have different letters that are adjacent and have the same number equivalent.) Pfeiffer, for example, is coded P160. Because the *P* and the *F* are both coded as 1, only one (*P*) is used. The letters *e* and *i* separate the coded *Pf* from the second and third appearance of the letter *f*, so one of these is coded. The double *f*'s again require that only one be considered in the code. The letter *r* is represented by 6, and in the absence of additional consonants, the code is rounded off with a zero. Other examples of double-letter names are Lennon (L550), Kelly (K400), Buerck (B620), Lloyd (L300), Schaefer (S160), Szucs (S200), and Orricks (O620). Occasionally the indexers themselves made mistakes in coding names, so it may be useful to look for a name in another code.

Different Names Within a Single Code

With this indexing formula, many different surnames may be included within the same Soundex code. For example, the similar-sounding surnames Scherman, Schurman, Sherman, Shireman, and Shurman are indexed together as S655 and will appear in the same group with other surnames, such as Sauerman or Sermon. Names that do not sound alike may also be included within a single code: Sinclair, Singler, Snegolski, Snuckel, Sanislo, San Miguel, Sungaila, and Szmegalski are all coded as S524.

Alphabetical Arrangement of First
or Given Names Within the Code

As described above, multiple surnames appear within most Soundex codes. Within each Soundex code, the individual and family cards are arranged alphabetically by given name. Marked divider cards separate most Soundex codes.

Mixed Codes

Divider cards show most code numbers, but not all. For instance, one divider may be numbered 350 and the next one 400. Between the two divided cards there may be names coded 353, 350, 360, 365, and 355, but instead of being in numerical order they are interfiled alphabetically by given name.

Soundex Reference Guide

For those who are unsure of their Soundex skills, most genealogical libraries have a copy of Bradley W. Steuart's *The Soundex Reference Guide: Soundex Codes to Over 125,000 Surnames.*

Soundex Abbreviations

In addition to the letter/numerical codes, Soundex also uses a number of abbreviations, most of which relate to residents' relationships to the head of the household. NR (not recorded) is a frequently found abbreviation.

Native Americans, Asians, and Nuns

Names of nuns, Native Americans, and Asians pose special problems. Phonetically spelled Asian and Native American names were either coded as one continuous name or by what seemed to be a surname. For example, the Native American name Shinka-Wa-Sa may have been coded as Shinka (S520) or Sa (S000). Nuns were coded as if "Sister" were the surname, and they appear in each state's Soundex under the code S236, but not necessarily in alphabetical order.

Soundex Research Tips

The Soundex indexes can be especially useful for identifying family units, because all members of the household are listed on the Soundex cards under the name of the head of the household. Often, census searches begin with only a surname and the name of the state in which a person or family lived in a given census year. In such cases, the Soundex can be a means of determining surname distribution throughout the state. Your search can then be narrowed to a smaller geographic area within a state. Once the county of origin is determined through census work, whole new paths of research open up. The Soundex can also be used to locate orphaned children living with persons of other surnames and to identify families with grandparents living under the same roof. They are sometimes listed on the Soundex cards, even though they may not be indexed separately.

CATALOGS

Four catalogs produced by the National Archives Trust Fund Board are especially helpful for conducting searches in federal census records. These catalogs are available in most archives and libraries that hold census microfilm. The Family History Library, however, maintains a different numbering system for cataloging the census records.

The *1790-1890 Federal Population Censuses: Catalog of the National Archives Microfilm* is arranged by state or territory and then by county. The series number and the total number of microfilm rolls in the enumeration is given for each microfilm publication. The catalog further identifies each microfilm roll by number and contents.

The *1900 Federal Population Census: A Catalog of Microfilm Copies of the Schedules* lists 1,854 rolls of microfilm on which the 1900 population census schedules appear. Numbers for the 7,846 rolls of the 1900 Soundex indexes appear in the second half of the book. The catalog is arranged by state or territory and then by county.

The *1910 Federal Population Census: A Catalog of Microfilm Copies of the Schedules* lists the 1,784 rolls of microfilm on which the 1910 population census schedules appear. Numbers for the

4,642 rolls of the 1910 Soundex/Miracode indexes appear in the second half of the catalog.

The *1920 Federal Population Census: Catalog of National Archives Microfilm* lists the 8,585 rolls of the 1920 Soundex indexes in the front portion of the book and 2,076 rolls of the 1920 census schedules arranged by state or territory and then by county.

Each catalog may be purchased for a small fee from the National Archives Trust Fund, NEPS Dept. 735, P.O. Box 100793, Atlanta, GA 30384.

MILITARY RECORDS

Military and pension records are among the most useful sources available to genealogists because of the detail they offer. These records are important because they may provide an ancestor's date of birth, place of residence, the names and addresses of family members, and other details that can round out a picture of his or her life.

JUDITH PROWSE REID
Head, Local History and Genealogy, Library of Congress
In *U.S. Military Records:*
A Guide to Federal and State Sources

Military records have originated at the federal, state, and local levels. Whether created in time of war or in time of peace, these records provide unique facts and insights into the lives of men and women who have served in the military forces of the United States. Almost every American family, in one generation or another, has seen one or more of its members serve in America's armed forces. From regimental histories, which provide blow-by-blow accounts of a unit's participation in military actions, to the personal details contained in the service and pension files of individual men and women, military records provide valuable information concerning a large and significant portion of the American population. And because military records have been preserved and made available at and through a number of research institutions, much information awaits the well-prepared researcher.

How to Find Military Records

To locate military records for any individual, it is essential to know when and where in the armed forces he or she served and whether that person served in the enlisted ranks or was an officer. (If you don't have that identifying information, some potential solutions are discussed below.)

As in any research project, it is important to study carefully whatever is already known about the subject of interest. Families and communities frequently pass down stories of military heroes from generation to generation. In most cases, these stories retain some fact, but, with the passage of years and in the process of retelling, accuracy fades. At any rate, family stories should not be overlooked for clues at the start of a military search.

When and where did the individual live? Did the family keep evidence of military service? Certificates, letters, journals, diaries, scrapbooks, newspaper clippings, photographs, medals, swords, and other memorabilia kept in private collections may provide the basic facts needed to begin searching in military record collections.

Military Time Lines

Creating a historical time line can be especially useful for determining if and when the subject might have served in the military. By compiling a chronological list of the known dates and places of residence of an individual from birth through adulthood, it is frequently easy to discover the possibility of military service. Was the individual the right age to be eligible for the draft or to serve voluntarily in the Civil War? Is it likely that the person served on the Northern rather than the Southern side, or vice versa? For records from the colonial period to more recent military engagements, the place of residence is key to finding an individual's records.

Evidence of Military Service in Hometown Records

There are a number of public records that are potentially valuable in discovering the military history of a veteran. It has been a long-standing American tradition to foster patriotism by honoring local sons and daughters who have defended the ideals of their country. Hometown military heroes are frequently noted on public monuments, and local newspaper files may yield surprisingly detailed accounts of a community's well-known and less-famous military personnel.

Military History

Commercial enterprises and historically oriented groups and institutions have regularly published local histories. As a rule, these histories will include glowing accounts of the area's involvement in military activities. Some volumes provide bio-

graphical sketches of military leaders, while others attempt to list all of the community's participants in various military conflicts. Locally focused histories have been published at various times for virtually every state and county in the United States. Do not overlook them as an important research aid. P. William Filby's *A Bibliography of American County Histories* is a list of five thousand such sources.

In addition to the standard histories, local public libraries and historical societies usually preserve and make available other types of publications that document the military history of the geographical areas they serve. Historical agencies collect biographies, letters, diaries, journals, and all sorts of memorabilia from military units and servicemen and -women. The personal accounts found in some collections are a fascinating means of stepping back in time. Firsthand accounts afford a better understanding of the day-to-day drudgery, loneliness, fears, and satisfactions of military life.

Evidence of Military Service in Cemeteries

Cemeteries provide yet another local source of information regarding individuals who served in the armed forces. Almost every cemetery in the United States contains some evidence of military events and veterans. Cemetery records and grave markers frequently identify military dead by name, rank, and unit designation. If a man or woman died elsewhere while in the service, the body was frequently brought home for burial; cemetery records often note the place and date of death.

Evidence of Military Service in Court Records

Court records are yet another potential source for identifying those who served in the military. Most counties formally recorded and indexed the names of their citizens who were discharged from the military. In some local courts, "military discharges" will be found indexed separately, and in others the military records may be oddly interspersed with deeds, naturalizations, or other categories of documents. The contents of military records may vary greatly from one courthouse to another. Some will provide biographical information, while others may simply list names and the event or names and date of certificate issue.

Military Records in the National Archives

Federal military documents that have been classified as archival material are in the custody of the National Archives and Records Administration. Not all records created by military agencies are judged to be permanently valuable. Generally, only records of historical or administrative importance are kept.

A wonderful array of federal military records are available in major libraries and archives and through microfilm rental programs. (Heritage Quest, a division of AGLL, Inc., P.O. Box 329, Bountiful, UT 84011-0329, is a source of rental microfilms.) With sufficient identifying information, you may request a search of the registers of enlistments or the compiled military service records. The minimum information required for a search is (1) the soldier's full name, (2) the war in which he or she served or period of service, and (3) the state from which he or she served. For the Civil War, you must also indicate whether the person served in Union or Confederate forces. A separate copy of the form must be used for military service, pension, and bounty-land warrant applications. Submit requests for information about individuals who served in the military before World War I on NATF form 80 (Order for Copies of Veterans Records). Write to the National Archives and Records Administration, General Reference Branch, Washington, DC 20408 to obtain copies of NATF form 80. Always ask for "all records" for an individual.

Make requests for information about U.S. Army officers separated from the service after 1912 on standard form 180 (Request Pertaining to Military Records) and send it to the Military Personnel Records Center, 9700 Page Boulevard, St. Louis, MO 63132.

U.S. Military Records

By far the most comprehensive study of military records and how to use them is found in James C. Neagles's *U.S. Military Records: A Guide to Federal and State Sources, Colonial America to the Present*. Neagles's guide addresses primary and secondary military sources and accessibility, including the following information-rich sources:

    Records of state militias and the National Guard
    Records of the army, navy, and other branches
        of the U.S. military
    Records of the military academies
    Post-service records
    Pensions
    Bounty-land grants
    Bonuses and family assistance

Soldier's homes
Military burials
Military installations
Censuses of veterans
Conscription
Civilian affairs
Family History Library, Genealogical Society of Utah
Military resources of the National Archives in
    Washington, D.C.
Resources of the National Archives repositories outside
    Washington, D.C., including:
National Archives II
National Personnel Records Center
National Archives regional archives
United States Army Military History Institute
U.S. Army Center of Military History
Office of Air Force History
Naval Historical Center
Marine Corps Historical Center
Coast Guard Historian's Office
Library of the National Guard Association of the United
    States
American Battle Monuments Commission
National Museum of Health and Medicine
Department of Veterans Affairs
Library of Congress
Headquarters and Library of the National Society of the
    Daughters of the American Revolution
Archdiocese for the Military Services
Air Force Historical Research Agency
United States Naval Institute
United States Military Academy Archives
Unites States Naval Academy Archives
Unites States Naval Academy Special Collections
    Division

United States Coast Guard Academy
United States Merchant Marine Academy
United States Air Force Academy
National Park Service Battle Sites

A state-by-state listing of military sources that are available in state archives and historical societies.

IMMIGRATION

Historians have proposed several reasons for [the] new and widespread interest in family history. The most frequently proposed reason is that, following the massive emigration from Europe to new lands, such as the Americas, there has been a breakdown in family bonds and a consequent loss of a sense of belonging among the descendants of the immigrants. Genealogy is the path to discovering our origins and reestablishing those family bonds.

TRAFFORD R. COLE
In *Italian Genealogical Records: How to Use Italian Civil, Ecclesiastical, and Other Records in Family History Research*

Since the First Naturalization Act of 26 March 1790 (1 Stat. 103), citizenship records have been kept by the federal government. However, it was not until 1820 that the federal government began to keep track of incoming ship passengers. Their exceptionally high research value make naturalization records and passenger lists among the most frequently used federal records.

We are all descended from immigrants. Whether they came to America in prehistoric times via the Bering Strait or later on ships or airplanes, at some point in history, every person's ancestors came from somewhere else. And almost everyone has a strong desire to know why, when, and from where their ancestors emigrated. Most of us begin with the simple goal of finding "old country" origins. Yet the quest usually does not end when that discovery is made. Once we begin tracking ancestors back in time and across continents, we are often drawn so deeply into the story that it's difficult to stop searching. There are always a few more relationships to be proved and details to

be learned. And when finally discovered, the ancestor's homeland takes on a fascination of its own. We find ourselves intrigued with histories and cultures, wanting to know as much as possible about "our people." Scarcely any phase of family history research is as fascinating as tracking immigrant origins—and scarcely any phase is quite as challenging.

How to Find Immigrant Origins

Knowing the immigrant's birthplace or last place of residence before emigrating is essential to finding more information in the native land. Yet, unless the ancestors arrived relatively recently in the United States, family origins may have been forgotten. Because most foreign records are kept at the town level, discovering the name of a native town, county, or parish is an

[Facsimile of a historical passenger list document titled "District of the City of New York, Port of New York" containing handwritten passenger names including Edgar B. Dawson, Dave Aaron, Bruno Kniffler, Rud. Ed. G. Pierron, Geo. McPhee, J. W. Stallmann, Mrs. C. M. Reed, F. G. Prentiss, Gerald Pigon, Henry Dätsch, Mrs. Edith Kinekamp, Mr. Josef Petkaroff, with columns for age, sex, calling or occupation, country of citizenship, native country, last residence, etc.]

important goal. Without that information, it is impossible to know where to conduct research in the country of origin.

Identify the Immigrant

To clearly identify an immigrant in records of the country from which the person came, you must know the person's full name, an approximate birth date, and the country of origin. Family stories, traditions, and heirlooms are wonderful starting points.

Surprising clues may survive in letters, diaries, journals, religious records, postcards, photographs, scrapbooks, and mementos that have been saved over the years.

Family members, friends, and neighbors often traveled to the United States together. If you can't find your immediate ancestor, it can be worthwhile to look for others whose records may lead you to sources that will include information on your own relative.

Records created by religious organizations comprise a likely source of information in the country of origin. By learning the immigrant's religion, you can further identify him or her and gain clues to more-specific geographical origins. (See chapter 7, "Foreign, Ethnic, and Religious Research.")

Ethnicity

The natural security of living among people who speak the same language and have the same cultural or religious background is the binding force that has traditionally kept ethnic communities together. Immigrants, particularly those who did not speak English, tended to settle in enclaves within cities and to cluster in specific regions of the United States. It was common for immigrants arriving in large numbers to settle together on this side of the ocean, and then to migrate en masse within the United States. Immigrant groups frequently founded their own churches, synagogues, schools, banks, boarding houses, and other institutions.

Volumes have been written about virtually every ethnic group. Ethnic presses generated newspapers and histories that focused on specific communities. Many ethnic publications survive that can be invaluable for those who want to learn more about the lives

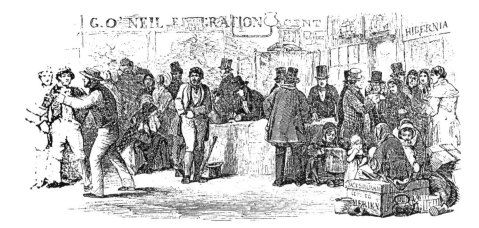

and times of their immigrant ancestors. Public libraries are the perfect starting places for a general search on an ethnic group, and the Internet is home to Web sites for almost every group.

NATURALIZATION RECORDS

Many immigrants became American citizens within a few years after their arrival in the United States. Most pre-1906 papers indicate the country (sometimes the province) of immigrant's origin. The Bureau of Immigration and Naturalization, created in 1906, began a system of uniformity, design, and control of forms. Beginning in September 1906, Immigration and Naturalization Service Form 2202 asked aliens for an exact date and place of birth, as well as for that person's last residence. The port of arrival in the United States and means of arrival (the name of the ship) were also included regularly after 1906. If an individual was married, he or she was required to provide the name and date and place of birth of the spouse. Form 2202 also required a list of children's names and the dates and places of their births.

SUZANNE MCVETTY
President of the Genealogical Speakers Guild
Columnist for *Ancestry* magazine

Naturalization is the legal procedure by which an alien becomes a citizen of a state or country. While citizenship documents are sought by family historians, both for their sentimental and for their informational value, these records are often hard to find and misunderstood.

About Naturalization Records and How to Find Them

- To begin the search for an immigrant's origins, try to learn as much as you can about that person, including full name, approximate birth date, native country, approximately when he or she came to the United States, and where that person lived after his or her arrival here.

• Since 1790, naturalizations in the United States have been performed according to federal law.

• Before 1906, any federal, state, or local court of record (a court having a seal or a record) could naturalize aliens.

• Generally, the best place to begin a naturalization search is in the county in which the immigrant settled in the U.S.

• There are some major indexes of naturalizations that took place in federal and local courts (created by the WPA) that can expedite searches for individuals who lived in the New England States, southern New York, and parts of several midwestern states. The microfilmed indexes are available in some of the regional archives of the National Archives and from the Family History Library, among other places.

• Many federal and local court naturalizations and naturalization indexes have been microfilmed and are available from the Family History Library.

• Aliens intending to be naturalized citizens first filed a declaration of intention to become a citizen.

• Declarations of intention are instruments by which applicants for U.S. citizenship renounced allegiance to foreign sovereignties and declared their intentions to become U.S. citizens.

• A declaration of intention usually preceded proof of residence or a petition to become a citizen by two or more years.

- In most years, a declaration of intention was not required if the citizen had an honorable discharge from the U.S. military or had entered the country when a minor (under the age of twenty-one).

- After five years in the United States (except for a brief period when the laws changed), an alien could petition a court to be naturalized.

- Naturalization petitions are instruments by which those who declared their intention to become a U.S. citizen and who had met the residence requirements made formal application for U.S. citizenship.

- Many aliens waited more than the required five years to become naturalized.

- Many aliens who filed declarations of intention never completed the process by petitioning for naturalization.

- Naturalization depositions are formal statements in support of an applicant's petition by witnesses designated by the applicant.

- Certificates or records of naturalization and oaths of allegiance are documents which granted citizenship to petitioners.

- Courts held hearings on the petitions of aliens and took testimony from witnesses to determine whether the alien met residence and character requirements.

- When the petition was accepted, the alien took the oath of allegiance and the court recorded the final order or certificate.

- Before 1906, the final order was usually recorded in the court's minute or order book, and the court usually issued the new citizen a certificate of naturalization.

- Before 1906, naturalization forms (records) often varied significantly from state to state, county to county, court to court, and from year to year.

- Between 1855 and 1922, an alien woman became a citizen automatically if she married an American citizen.

- A woman could derive citizenship from her naturalized father or her husband (derivative citizenship).

- Relatively few single women became naturalized citizens before 1922, and married women could not be naturalized on their own unless they were widowed or divorced.

- Non-native minor children became American citizens when their parents were naturalized.

- Former black slaves were made citizens by the ratification of the Fourteenth Amendment to the U.S. Constitution, 1868.

- American Indians were made citizens by federal laws passed in 1887 and 1924.

- Aliens from China, Japan, and other East and South Asian countries were barred from becoming citizens from 1882 to 1943.

- Expedited naturalization proceedings have been available to aliens who were army veterans since 1862; navy veterans since 1894; and wartime enlisted servicemen and women since 1918.

- Under the 1906 Basic Naturalization Act, naturalization forms were standardized and the U.S. Bureau of Immigration and Naturalization, later the Immigration and Naturalization Service (INS), examined petitions for naturalization.

- After 1906, there is more biographical information on the standardized naturalization records.

- The INS has duplicate naturalization records for individuals who were naturalized after 1906.

- Women twenty-one years of age or over were entitled to citizenship in 1922, and derivative citizenship was discontinued.

- While this brief description will get you started, there is a more complete study of the records in Loretto Dennis Szucs's *They Became Americans: Finding Naturalization Records and Ethnic Origins.*

PASSENGER ARRIVAL LISTS

Over four hundred years, from the 1500s through the 1900s, they came to America in the millions...our ancestors! From Europe, Africa, and Asia, from Central and South America, they came in ships—steamships and sailing vessels arriving along the shores of the Atlantic, the Pacific, the Gulf of Mexico, and the Great Lakes. And millions of these immigrant arrivals are recorded in surviving ship passenger lists.

JOHN P. COLLETTA, PH.D.
In *They Came in Ships: A Guide to Finding Your Immigrant Ancestor's Arrival Record*

What fires the imagination more than the image of our own immigrant ancestors first setting foot on American soil? Your family's arrival in the United States is an important part of your personal history. There may be a passenger arrival list that shows your ancestor's name—and hopefully a lot more about him or her. For most ships entering U.S. ports between 1565 and 1954, a passenger list was compiled. While not all passenger lists have survived, most extant lists include the name of the ship, the captain's name, the port and date of the ship's departure, and the port and date of arrival in the U.S. Additionally, passenger lists include a roster of the passengers with varying amounts of identifying information.

Passenger arrival lists can be among the most valuable sources for documenting our ancestors' immigration. While the content of passenger lists has changed significantly over the years, these much-sought records are in great demand by demographers, historians, genealogists, and even those with just a casual interest in their heritage.

Official U.S. government passenger arrival lists are available from 1820 (when the government first kept passenger lists) through 1945 for most of the ports in the United States with customs houses. Those available in the National Archives on microfilm are tabulated in *Immigration and Passenger Arrivals: A Select Catalog of National Archives Microfilms*. The lists are divided into customs passenger lists (original lists, copies, or abstracts) and immigration passenger lists (State Department transcripts and lists) with pertinent indexes. Microfilm copies are also available for searching at the Family History Library and its family history centers located throughout the United States. Selected passenger lists are available at some public and genealogical libraries. The Allen County Public Library in Fort Wayne, Indiana, for example, has a large collection of passenger list microfilms.

For pre-1820 official lists, researchers must rely on surviving ship cargo manifests. Many colonial and U.S. ports kept copies of manifests filed as a requirement for clearance. The existing

manifests have been scattered among archives, museums, and other historical agencies, but most have been reproduced in published form and are indexed in P. William Filby's *Passenger and Immigration Lists Index*.

While at least some passenger lists have been indexed for virtually every U.S. port, a large number remain unindexed. As with other government documents, passenger lists were not intended to be genealogical documents, but rather were a means of monitoring immigrant arrivals. Historically, up to seven different passenger lists were created and perhaps more for some groups of passengers. These include lists made and filed with:

The port of embarkation
Ports of call along the route
The port of arrival
Newspapers at the port of departure
Newspapers at the cities of arrival
A copy kept with or as part of the ship's manifest
Notations in the ship's log

Federal control brought about the creation of several types of passenger arrival records. All of them are available for searching, with some restrictions. A thorough discussion of the nature and history of U.S. passenger lists is in Michael Tepper's *American Passenger Arrival Records*. A succinct guide to using those lists and the available indexes is John P. Colletta's *They Came in Ships: A Guide to Finding Your Immigrant Ancestor's Arrival Record*.

One of the most significant developments in genealogy in the past fifteen years has been the publication of indexes to immigration passenger lists. The largest project is Filby's *Passenger and Immigration Lists Index*, which contains more than 2 million entries for immigrants from the British Isles and Europe.

LAND RECORDS

Prior to the Civil War, more than eighty-five percent of all Americans owned or leased land. Therefore, almost every researcher, whether a seasoned professional or weekend hobbyist, has required land records to document the existence, association, or movement of an individual or ancestral family. While many researchers may feel a sense of historical excitement when finding an ancestor in a land deed, many also fail to understand the importance of such a document and how land can be used to make vital links between generations; they are not aware that it can bridge distant origins and help solve even the most difficult problems.

E. WADE HONE
In *Land and Property Research in the United States*

The right to own land has always been one of the great incentives for living in the United States. Yet researchers often overlook the importance of land records as a source of family history information. Written evidence of people's entitlement goes back in time further than virtually any other type of record family historians might use.

Land records meet the needs of researchers in different ways and contain a variety of genealogical and historical data. They are a major source of information for many family histories and provide primary source material for local history as well. They are closely related to probate and other official court records and should be investigated in connection with them. Land and property are leading issues in the settlement of estates, and the majority of civil cases in the courts deal with real and personal property. Although land records rarely yield vital statistics, in many instances they provide the only proof of family relationships. Often they include the names of heirs of an estate (including daughters' married names and a widow's subsequent married name) and refer to related probates and other court cases by number and court name. In some places where other records are scarce, the land records take on extra importance. Occasionally these documents disclose former residences and more often provide the new address of the grantors or heirs at the time of the sale of the property.

Land records provide two types of important evidence for the family historian. First, they often document family relationships. Second, they place individuals in a specific time and place, allowing the researcher to sort people and families into neighborhoods and closely related groups. One of land records' most important qualities is that they are sometimes the only records that allow us to distinguish one person of a common name from another.

Land Records in the National Archives
The National Archives has bounty-land warrant files, donation land entry files, homestead application files, and private land claim files relating to the entry of individual settlers on land in the public land states. There are no land records for the original thirteen states or for Maine, Vermont, West Virginia, Kentucky, Tennessee, Texas, and Hawaii. Records for these states are maintained by state officials, usually in the state capital. Searching for the record of a particular land grant from the federal government requires contacting both the Bureau of Land Management (BLM) and the National Archives (NARA). As of 1996, the BLM is divided into eastern and western states. Records for the eastern states are at the Eastern States Office, 7450 Boston Boulevard, Springfield, VA 22153. Most of the western states have their own offices. Information on land records in the National Archives can be obtained by writing to the National Archives and Records Administration,

Washington, DC 20408. See more on land records in chapter 4, "Local Records"; and see chapter 10, "Family History, Computers, and the Internet" for more information on obtaining information from the National Archives.

HOMESTEAD RECORDS

The United States Congress passed the Homestead Act in May of 1862. Generally, this act gave a citizen (or an alien intending to become a citizen) 160 acres of land, free of charge, if certain requirements were met. Usually, applicants had to build a home on the land, cultivate it, and reside there for five years. Homesteading had a profound effect on the nation. It is estimated that between 400,000 and 600,000 families were provided with new farms as a result of the original act and amendments.

MICHAEL JOHN NEILL,
Genealogical Instructor
In *Ancestry* magazine

As E. Wade Hone notes in *Land and Property Research in the United States,*"[The purpose of the Homestead Law] was to distribute public lands to those who were without" (page 140). The law sought to lure large numbers of immigrants who had settled in urban areas to less-developed areas of the United States. With the passage of the Homestead Act, individuals began filing claims as early as 1 January 1863. While the majority of the claims were completed between 1863 and 1917, the law was not abolished until 1976.

When an individual found a desired piece of land, it was necessary to file a claim for the chosen property. This was accomplished in person through the local land office or directly at the General Land Office in Washington, D.C. It is the claim process that provides records of interest to family historians. Completed homestead entry papers usually include the homestead application, the certificate of publication of intention to make a claim, the homestead proof, testimony of two witnesses and the claimant, and the final certificate. Also included, when applicable, were naturalization papers and discharge papers from the Union Army.

Homestead records are available only through the National Archives in Washington, D.C. Unfortunately, there is no master index to the records. Original files are organized by land office and final certificate number, so it is essential to know where the process began. Evidence of homestead patents is sometimes found in the possession of descendants of homesteaders, or in county-level deed records.

RECORDS ABOUT NATIVE AMERICANS

Begin Native American research, like any other family history investigation, with home sources, and interview family members who may remember important names, dates, places, and tribal affiliation. These answers are usually the richest and most valuable sources of information, and the basis to begin research in outside sources.

Some family stories allude only to "Indian ancestry." However, it is essential to identify the tribe from which you are descended in order to pursue actual records. Once the specific tribe is identified, it is advisable to learn as much as possible about that tribe, giving special attention to the family unit, naming and marriage customs, and the relationship system of the tribe. Some knowledge of tribal origins, migration patterns, and how and where the federal government removed (relocated) tribes is critical to discovering Native American family history. Good bibliographies of Native American sources are available through most public libraries.

The National Archives has many records relating to Indians who maintained their tribal affiliation. The original records of the headquarters of the Bureau of Indian Affairs are in the National Archives in Washington, D.C. These records often contain information about specific tribal members. Original records created by the various field offices and Indian schools are among the holdings of the National Archives' regional archives. Most of the records are arranged by tribe and date from 1830 to 1940. Among the records most useful to family historians are special Indian census lists, enrollment records, and allotment records.

A useful guide is Edward E. Hill's *Guide to Records in the National Archives of the United States Relating to American Indians* (Washington, D.C.: National Archives and Records Administration, 1981). Curt B. Witcher and George J. Nixon offer guidelines for Indian research, a discussion of especially helpful records and what they contain, a list of select tribes (including where records are located), and an extensive bibliography for Indian research in "Tracking Native American Family History" in *The Source: A Guidebook of American Genealogy.*

U.S. SOCIAL SECURITY DEATH INDEX

> *The federal government is one of the largest creators of records in the United States. One of the most important collections of information is kept by the Social Security Administration. Charged with providing Social Security benefits to all eligible citizens, the agency has had to keep track of millions of Americans. While their records of living persons are protected by rights of privacy, records of deceased persons are available.*
>
> KORY L. MEYERINK
> *Printed Sources: A Guide to*
> *Published Genealogical Records*

Since President Franklin D. Roosevelt signed the Social Security Act into law in 1935, nearly 400 million Social Security cards have been issued. The Social Security Administration has developed the Social Security Death Master File, ranked as one of the largest computer databases with genealogical application. Though it includes nearly 60 million entries, the Social Security Death Index (SSDI) cannot be considered a complete index to American deaths. The vast majority of the entries included in the SSDI are related to benefits distributed at or before the death of the person listed. Close to 98 percent of the SSDI represents individuals who have died after 1962, when the database was started.

The major advantage of the SSDI is that it is a way to find death dates and places of death for family members whose whereabouts may be unknown. For some, the SSDI may be the critical clue needed to discover information about relatives as close as parents or grandparents. People who were adopted or have lost contact with family members often find this source to be one of the only ways that they can begin an investigation. For those who don't actually need the information from SSDI, the records may provide just another source of documentation or proof, or just add another interesting dimension to the family story. It is also wise to track records of uncles, aunts, or other relatives whose records may also lead back to a common ancestor. The SSDI is often a steppingstone to other records, such as obituaries, cemetery records, and official death records. Once the exact date and place of death are determined from the SSDI, any number of sources can be investigated.

The Family History Library has added the Social Security database to its *FamilySearch®* collection on CD-ROM, and Ancestry and several other companies have made the Social Security Death Index available in CD-ROM format. The disc allows you to search for potential ancestors whose names may appear in this mammoth index. The database is updated periodically. You may search by surname, given name, state of last residence, birth year, or death year. For nearly every name you find you can view the following information: birth date, death date, Social Security number, and the date on which the individual's Social Security card was issued. The Social Security Death Index is also available without charge at the Ancestry.com Web site (http://www.ancestry.com).

The Freedom of Information Act has made available copies of the original applications of those Social Security card holders who have died. There is a fee of $7.00 if the Social Security number is known, $16.50 if the number is unknown or incorrect. Copies are available from:

Social Security Administration
Freedom of Information Officer.
4-H-8 Annex Building
6401 Security Blvd.
Baltimore, MD 21235

SELECTED READING

Ancestry Reference Library. CD-ROM. Salt Lake City: Ancestry, 1998.

Anuta, Michael J. *Ships of Our Ancestors.* Baltimore: Genealogical Publishing Co., 1993.

Colletta, John P. *They Came in Ships: A Guide to Finding Your Immigrant Ancestor's Arrival Record.* Rev.ed. Salt Lake City: Ancestry, 1993.

Eichholz, Alice, ed. *Ancestry's Red Book: American State, County and Town Sources.* Rev. ed. Salt Lake City: Ancestry, 1992.

Filby, P. William. *A Bibliography of American County Histories.* Baltimore: Genealogical Publishing Co., 1985.

Filby, P. William, and Mary K. Meyer. *Passenger and Immigration Lists Index.* Detroit: Gale Research Co., 1981–.

Hone, E. Wade. *Land and Property Research in the United States.* Salt Lake City: Ancestry, 1997.

Immigration and Passenger Arrivals: A Select Catalog of National Archives Microfilms. Rev. ed. Washington, D.C.: National Archives Trust Fund, 1991.

National Archives and Records Administration. *Guide to Genealogical Research in the National Archives.* Rev. ed. Washington, DC: National Archives Trust Fund Board, 1985.

Neagles, James C. *U.S. Military Records: A Guide to Federal and State Sources, Colonial America to the Present.* Salt Lake City: Ancestry, 1994.

Steuart, Bradley W. *The Soundex Reference Guide: Soundex Codes to Over 125,000 Surnames.* Bountiful, Utah: Precision Indexing, 1990.

Szucs, Loretto Dennis. *They Became Americans: Finding Naturalization Records and Ethnic Origins.* Salt Lake City: Ancestry, 1998.

Szucs, Loretto Dennis, and Sandra Hargreaves Luebking, eds. *The Archives: A Guide to the National Archives Field Branches.* Salt Lake City: Ancestry, 1988. Also available on CD-ROM as part of Ancestry Reference Library (Salt Lake City: Ancestry, 1997).

————, eds. *The Source: A Guidebook of American Genealogy.* Rev. ed. Salt Lake City: Ancestry, 1997.

Tepper, Michael H. *American Passenger Arrival Records: A Guide to the Records of Immigrants Arriving at American Ports by Sail and Steam.* Updated and enl. ed. Baltimore: Genealogical Publishing Co., 1993.

Microfilm copies of census, immigration, and many other federal records are available on loan from Heritage Quest (formerly AGLL), P.O. Box 329, Bountiful, UT 84011-0329.

Also see the Social Security Death Index on CD-ROM (Salt Lake City: Ancestry, 1996) and at http://www.ancestry.com. It indexes the Social Security Death Master File, which lists all individuals who have received a Social Security card and are reported as deceased.

The Ancestry Reference Library CD-ROM (Salt Lake City: Ancestry, 1998) contains ten reference works that list and describe federal and other records useful for genealogy research.

Chapter Four

$\mathcal{L}$OCAL $\mathcal{R}$ECORDS

VITAL RECORDS

Vital records, as their name suggests, are connected with central life events: birth, marriage, and death. Maintained by civil authorities, they are prime sources of genealogical information. These records, despite their recent creation in the United States, are critically important in genealogical research, often supplying details on family members well back into the nineteenth century.

Many British and European countries began keeping birth and death records nationally in the nineteenth century. Before then, churches maintained registers of christenings and burials, and colonial settlers in America brought British laws and customs with them. Thus, churches were initially the sole keepers of vital records; ministers in many colonies were required by law to report christenings and burials to civil authorities. In some areas, consequently, these events are recorded in both civil and church records. Eventually, some colonies, primarily those in New England, passed laws requiring local town or county clerks to maintain records of births and deaths.

JOHNI CERNY
"Research in Birth, Death, and Cemetery Records"
In *The Source: A Guidebook of American Genealogy*

In most cases, after you've searched the sources discussed in the preceding chapters, vital records (births, marriages, deaths) are the most easily accessible sources. Every state and county has a division responsible for maintaining and dispersing information from its vital record holdings. This division is usually known as the Bureau of Vital Records or the Department of Health, and it is often located in the state capital.

Vital records are often stepping stones to finding other records. In addition to an individual's full name, the date of the event recorded, and the person's residence at the time of the event, vital records sometimes provide other biographical data, such as parents' names and their birthplaces. As in every other aspect of genealogical research, the records of siblings, cousins, aunts and uncles, and even distant relatives can be very important. When a particular record does not contain helpful information, or when a record for an individual can't be found at all, the record of another relative may provide the needed clues that will lead back to the common ancestor. For example, the death record of one person may state that the parents' birthplaces are unknown, while the death record of his or her sibling may well include that missing information. Each vital record has the potential of taking you back one more generation with new names.

The United States was comparatively late in requiring vital statistics registration. In fact, the majority of the states did not implement registration until the first quarter of the twentieth century, and then the responsibility for registering births and deaths was left to the individual states rather than the federal government, accounting for different starting dates of vital record-keeping and the unevenness of information provided in vital records. In order to monitor medical statistics, such as infant mortality and epidemic diseases, many cities required registration earlier than the states. Fourteen states initiated registration before 1880. The earliest cities to require civil registration were New Orleans (1790), Boston (1848), Philadelphia (1860), Pittsburgh (1870), and Baltimore (1875).

Begin your search for vital records at the county level by writing or visiting the record-keeping agency for the county in which the event occurred. You may be asked to provide some identification. Some states and counties ask for proof of membership in a genealogical society to obtain the records, and in some it is necessary to state on the request form that the information received from the vital records office will be used "for genealogical purposes only." Birth records, especially those less than seventy-two years old, are protected by privacy laws and are often restricted because people have been known to use them to establish false identities. While access laws and copy fees differ from one state to another, almost all states have statewide indexes of vital registrations.

Forms for requesting birth, marriage, and death records that are issued by states and counties often ask for more information than you will be able to supply. Fill out forms as completely as possible, estimating dates as best you can. Most clerks will search indexes for a three- to five-year period; however, if they don't find the record immediately, some clerks will not search beyond the date supplied. Fees are usually not refunded when a record is not found.

Current search fees and addresses for all states are available from the vital records section of the health department of each state. In some instances, it is less expensive to purchase certificates directly from the county where the event took place. Certified copies are not required for genealogical documentation.

Thomas Jay Kemp's *International Vital Records Handbook* includes copies of application forms (which you may photocopy and use) for every state and provides addresses, telephone numbers, fees, and dates for which birth, marriage, and death records are available. This handbook is current as of the date of publication only; therefore, it is wise to telephone the state health department to verify the fee and address before ordering a certificate.

The Genealogical Society of Utah has microfilmed vital records of thousands of towns and counties throughout the United States. These microfilms are available at the Family History Library and upon request through its family history centers. (See chapter 18, "The Family History Library and Its Centers.")

COMPUTER SEARCHING

You may wish to conduct a preliminary search for vital records online. Some counties and states provide services for ordering vital records online. Indexes to some vital records for a few states are available through the office of the secretary of the state, through the state archives, or through the state genealogical society.

A significant number of early American vital records can be found in published form—in books, in CD-ROM format, and on the Internet. A number of early American vital records, for example, are available online through Ancestry.com. While indexes and printed sources can provide excellent leads, verify all new information by comparing it with original records and other sources if possible.

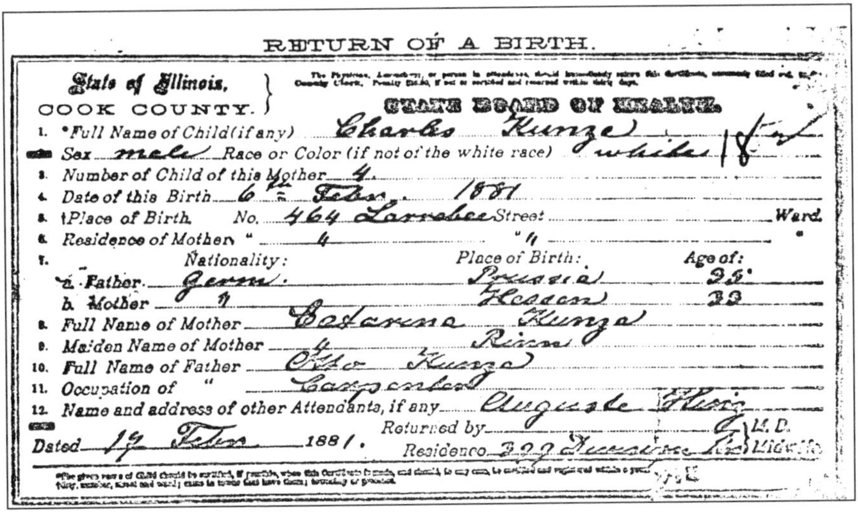
RETURN OF A BIRTH.

State of Illinois,
COOK COUNTY.

STATE BOARD OF HEALTH.

1. *Full Name of Child (if any) Charles Kunze
2. Sex male Race or Color (if not of the white race) white
3. Number of Child of this Mother 4.
4. Date of this Birth 6th Febr. 1881
5. †Place of Birth. No. 464 Larrabee Street Ward.
6. Residence of Mother " " "
7. Nationality: Place of Birth: Age of:
   a. Father Germ. Prussia 35
   b. Mother " Hessen 33
8. Full Name of Mother Catarina Kunze
9. Maiden Name of Mother "
10. Full Name of Father Otto Kunze
11. Occupation of " Carpenter
12. Name and address of other Attendants, if any Auguste

Dated 19 Febr. 1881. Returned by M.D.
Residence Midwife

Figure 4-1.

Birth Records

Most early birth records contain very little biographical information. Typical early New England town and church records, for example, give little information beyond the name of the child, date and place of birth, and parents' names. Some localities listed only the name of the father.

While early birth records can be discouragingly lacking in information, by the mid-nineteenth century birth records in the United States began to include more information. (See figure 4-1, 1881 Illinois birth record for Charles Kunze, and figure 4-2, 1901 New York birth record for Joseph Raymond Dennis.) Even though births were not widely recorded during the early years of America's existence, the records that do exist may be the only source of a birth date for an individual and should always be consulted.

Delayed births are also important vital registrations that you should consider for obtaining biographical information. When Social Security benefits were instituted in 1937, individuals claiming benefits had to document their birth even if the state

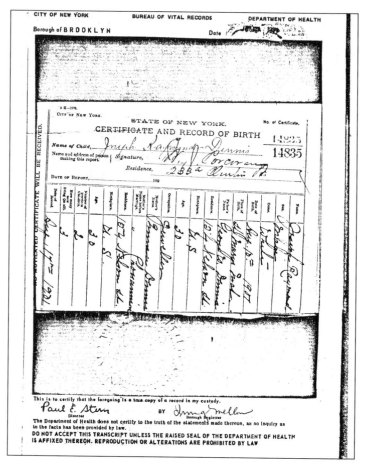

Figure 4-2.

of their birth did not require registration when they were born. Individuals who were not registered with state or county agencies at the time of their birth often applied for a delayed birth registration. Obtaining passports, insurance, and other benefits also required proof of age. Applications were accompanied with full name, address, and date and place of birth; father's name, race, and place of birth; and evidence to support the facts presented. The evidence could be in the form of a baptismal certificate, Bible record, school record, affidavit from the attending physician or midwife, application for an insurance policy, birth certificate of a child, or an affidavit from a person having definite knowledge of the facts. Delayed birth records are usually filed and indexed separately from regular birth registrations, and it may be necessary to request a separate search for them.

Death Records

Early death records in the United States provide little more than the name of the deceased, the date of death, and the place of death. Obituaries and cemetery, court, and other records

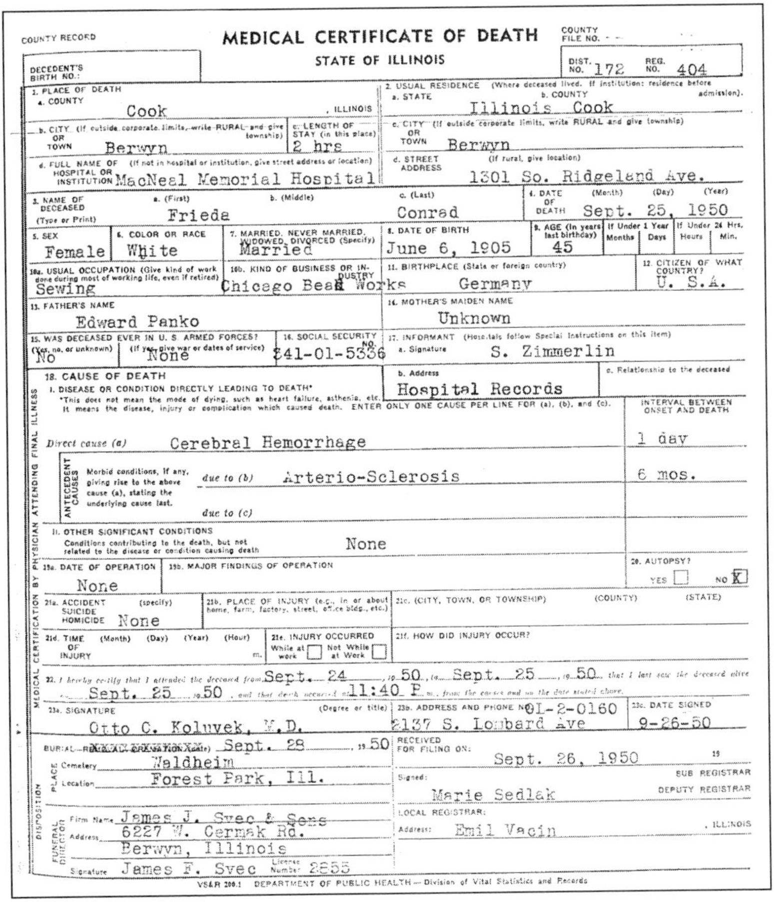
COUNTY RECORD
MEDICAL CERTIFICATE OF DEATH
STATE OF ILLINOIS
COUNTY FILE NO.
DECEDENT'S BIRTH NO.:
DIST. NO. 172 REG. NO. 404

1. PLACE OF DEATH a. COUNTY Cook, ILLINOIS
b. CITY OR TOWN (If outside corporate limits, write RURAL and give township) Berwyn
c. LENGTH OF STAY (in this place) 2 hrs
d. FULL NAME OF HOSPITAL OR INSTITUTION (If not in hospital or institution, give street address or location) MacNeal Memorial Hospital
2. USUAL RESIDENCE (Where deceased lived. If institution: residence before admission). a. STATE Illinois b. COUNTY Cook
c. CITY OR TOWN (If outside corporate limits, write RURAL and give township) Berwyn
d. STREET ADDRESS (If rural, give location) 1301 So. Ridgeland Ave.
3. NAME OF DECEASED (Type or Print) a. (First) Frieda b. (Middle) c. (Last) Conrad
4. DATE OF DEATH (Month) (Day) (Year) Sept. 25, 1950
5. SEX Female
6. COLOR OR RACE White
7. MARRIED, NEVER MARRIED, WIDOWED, DIVORCED (Specify) Married
8. DATE OF BIRTH June 6, 1905
9. AGE (In years last birthday) 45 If Under 1 Year Months Days If Under 24 Hrs. Hours Min.
10a. USUAL OCCUPATION (Give kind of work done during most of working life, even if retired) Sewing
10b. KIND OF BUSINESS OR INDUSTRY Chicago Bead Works
11. BIRTHPLACE (State or foreign country) Germany
12. CITIZEN OF WHAT COUNTRY? U. S. A.
13. FATHER'S NAME Edward Panko
14. MOTHER'S MAIDEN NAME Unknown
15. WAS DECEASED EVER IN U. S. ARMED FORCES? (Yes, no, or unknown) No (If yes, give war or dates of service) None
16. SOCIAL SECURITY NO. 341-01-5336
17. INFORMANT (Hospitals follow Special Instructions on this item) a. Signature S. Zimmerlin
b. Address Hospital Records
c. Relationship to the deceased
18. CAUSE OF DEATH
I. DISEASE OR CONDITION DIRECTLY LEADING TO DEATH* *This does not mean the mode of dying, such as heart failure, asthenia, etc. It means the disease, injury or complication which caused death. ENTER ONLY ONE CAUSE PER LINE FOR (a), (b), and (c).
INTERVAL BETWEEN ONSET AND DEATH
Direct cause (a) Cerebral Hemorrhage 1 day
ANTECEDENT CAUSES Morbid conditions, if any, giving rise to the above cause (a), stating the underlying cause last. due to (b) Arterio-Sclerosis 6 mos.
due to (c)
II. OTHER SIGNIFICANT CONDITIONS Conditions contributing to the death, but not related to the disease or condition causing death None
19a. DATE OF OPERATION None
19b. MAJOR FINDINGS OF OPERATION
20. AUTOPSY? YES ☐ NO ☒
21a. ACCIDENT SUICIDE HOMICIDE (specify) None
21b. PLACE OF INJURY (e.g., in or about home, farm, factory, street, office bldg., etc.)
21c. (CITY, TOWN, OR TOWNSHIP) (COUNTY) (STATE)
21d. TIME OF INJURY (Month) (Day) (Year) (Hour) m.
21e. INJURY OCCURRED While at Work ☐ Not While at Work ☐
21f. HOW DID INJURY OCCUR?
22. I hereby certify that I attended the deceased from Sept. 24, 1950, to Sept. 25, 1950, that I last saw the deceased alive on Sept. 25, 1950, and that death occurred at 11:40 P. m., from the causes and on the date stated above.
23a. SIGNATURE Otto C. Koluvek, M.D. (Degree or title)
23b. ADDRESS AND PHONE NO. 01-2-0160 2137 S. Lombard Ave
23c. DATE SIGNED 9-26-50
BURIAL, CREMATION, REMOVAL (Specify) (Date) Sept. 28, 1950
PLACE Cemetery Waldheim Location Forest Park, Ill.
RECEIVED FOR FILING ON: Sept. 26, 1950
Signed: Marie Sedlak SUB REGISTRAR DEPUTY REGISTRAR
LOCAL REGISTRAR: Address: Emil Vacin, ILLINOIS
FUNERAL DIRECTOR Firm Name James J. Svec & Sons Address 6227 W. Cermak Rd. Berwyn, Illinois
Signature James F. Svec License Number 2855
VS&R 200.1 DEPARTMENT OF PUBLIC HEALTH—Division of Vital Statistics and Records

Figure 4-3.

often provide more information about the deceased than do most official death records created before the last quarter of the 1800s.

By 1900 death records included more details. They often include the name of the deceased; date, place, and cause of death; age at the time of death; place of birth; parents' names; occupation; name of spouse; name of the person giving the information; the informant's relationship to the deceased; the name and address of the funeral director; and the place of burial. Race is listed in some records, and modern death certificates generally include a Social Security number. (Illinois Medical Certificate of Death for Frieda Conrad [figure 4–3]).

MARRIAGE RECORDS

Because of the importance of the legal distribution and control of property, most states and counties began to record marriages before births and deaths. The recording of a marriage is a two-step process. Traditionally, couples apply for a license to marry, and the applications are usually filed loose among other applications or in bound volumes. Marriage returns are filed once the marriage has taken place. The latter document is the proof of a marriage (not the license application).

Marriage applications are often filled out by both the bride and groom and typically contain a significant amount of genealogical information. They may list full names of the bride and groom, their residences, races, ages, dates and places of birth, previous marriages, occupations, and their parents' names, places of birth, and occupations.

Marriage certificates are issued by counties after the marriage ceremony is completed, and these are usually found among family items. While the certificates tend to have less biographical data than the application, the name of the individual officiating at the wedding may lead you to religious records by revealing the denomination. The religious records, in turn, may reveal the names of witnesses and other useful information.

Early American records sometimes include marriage bonds, which served as a protection for the future children of the marriage. A bond obligated a prospective groom to pay the bond if he were discovered to be a bigamist or imposter or otherwise ineligible to contract a valid marriage. As long as the marriage was legal, the bond was void. Bonds generally include the groom's name, name of the surety, the sum, and the date of the agreement.

COURT RECORDS

Even today, few people escape mention in court records at some time during their lives as witnesses, litigants, jurors, appointees to office, or as petition signatories. However, Americans of a few generations ago also expected to attend local court proceedings when they were in session.

ARLENE H. EAKLE, PH.D.
"Research in Court Records"
In *The Source: A Guidebook of American Genealogy*

American court files mirror U.S. history. Buried away in courthouses and archives everywhere are the dreams and frustrations of millions of citizens. The chances are great that your ancestors have left a detailed record of at least some aspects of their lives in court records.

Most of us don't think of court records as the rich source of personal history that they are. But America's English heritage established a tradition of court processes in which the people have a right to participate actively—and we always have. With relative freedom from royal supervision and with court enforcement of religious as well as civil laws, American courts tried many matters that were not subject to court action in other parts of the British empire and that are now considered too minor to warrant criminal action. According to Arlene Eakle in *The Source: A Guidebook of American Genealogy* (page 173), "In many places, until the Civil War, people were criminally prosecuted for such crimes as gossiping, witchcraft, scolding a husband, being publicly disrespectful to a minister, and refusing to attend church services."

PROBATE RECORDS

When a person dies, every state has laws that provide for public supervision over the estate that is left, whether or not there is a will. The term "probate records" broadly covers all the records produced by these laws, although, strictly speaking, "probate" applies only when there is a will.

> *Family history researchers often turn to probate records only after they have exhausted everything else they can find. Sometimes an earlier look at probate records would greatly shorten their search.*
>
> DONN DEVINE, JD, CG, CGI
> In *Ancestry* magazine

Family historians use probate case files far more than any other kind of court record. Probate case files are logical sources because they tend to include so much personal data, and because Americans have depended on the courts to settle their estates since North America was colonized. According to Val Greenwood in his *Researcher's Guide to American Genealogy*, "All records which relate to the disposition of an estate after its owner's death are referred to as probate records. These are many and varied in both content and value, but basically, they fall into two main classes: testate and intestate" (page 255). Probate case files generally provide names, addresses, and biographical data for the deceased, but frequently provide the same information for other relatives named in the papers. Relationships, maiden names of wives, married names of daughters, past residences, and place of origin in a native country are just a few of the details that can be discovered in probate files. And probate files can be found in courthouses and archives across the United States.

When requesting probate information from the county clerk, it is important not to limit yourself by asking for a person's "will." The clerk will usually take you at your word and not copy other papers in the probate file that may have equally important information if there is no will.

Even if your ancestor is not mentioned in a probate case, consider all of the other procedures which might have resulted in him or her appearing in court records:

Admiralty courts (concerning events that took place at sea, on lakes, etc.)
Adoptions
Affidavits
Apprenticeships
Bankruptcies
Bonds
Chancery
Civil cases
Civil War claims
Claims
Complaints
Court opinions
Criminal
Decrees
Declarations
Defendant

Depositions
Divorce
Dockets
Guardianship
Judgments
Jury records
Land disputes
Marshals' records
Military
Minutes
Naturalization records
Notices
Orders
Orphan records
Petitions
Plaintiff
Printed court records
Probate
Receipts
Slave and Slave owners
Subpoenas
Summons
Testimony
Transcripts
Witnesses

The above list is from "Research in Court Records" in *The Source: A Guidebook of American Genealogy*, rev. ed. (Salt Lake City: Ancestry, 1997).

CITY DIRECTORIES

Surprisingly, access is not a great problem with city directories. You can find city directories in almost every local library in the country, though larger libraries might have a greater variety. Go first to the public library nearest the place you are researching: if you can't travel there, telephone its reference desk. The reference librarian may be willing to photocopy the pages you need and send them to you or give you the desired information verbally.

GORDON LEWIS REMINGTON
"Research in Directories"
In *The Source: A Guidebook of American Genealogy*

An advantage of conducting research in any city or town is the availability of printed directories. There is scarcely a more satisfying or more productive adventure in family history research than finding an ancestor in an old city directory, thereby discovering his or her occupation (or multiple occupations) and exactly where in the city he or she lived. The enjoyment grows if you are able to track families for significant time periods. Almost all cities, large and small, had directories printed from their earliest days. To locate and use city directories most effectively, consult chapter 11, "Research in Directories," by Gordon Lewis Remington, in *The Source: A Guidebook of American Genealogy*.

CEMETERY RECORDS

The final resting place of your ancestors is an appropriate place to begin your search for information about their lives. From the gravestone itself you may learn the names, birth dates, and dates of death for persons buried there.

KAREN FRISCH
In *Unlocking the Secrets in Old Photographs*

Cemetery records and gravestone inscriptions are a rich source of information for family historians. Cemetery and other sources of information associated with death include:

Biographical works
Burial permits
Church burial registers
Cemetery records (often several different kinds are kept)
Cemetery indexes (often compiled by genealogical
    societies)
Cemetery sextons' records
Cemetery deed and plot registers
Death certificates
Death indexes
Family bibles
Family burial plots
Funeral director's records
Grave opening orders
Gravestone (monument) inscriptions
Military records
Monuments and memorials
Necrologies

Newspaper death notices
Obituaries
Probate records
Published death records
Religious records
Transcriptions of cemetery inscriptions

NEWSPAPERS

> The Wall Street Journal *once advertised itself as the "daily diary of the American dream." That statement, like much advertising copy, may have been somewhat overblown, but it does encapsulate much of the importance of newspapers to the genealogical researcher. Newspapers are, for those who become proficient in their use, the day-to-day (or week-to-week) diaries of local community events. They are thus excellent sources for family history, giving accounts of events from a contemporary point of view and often including details recorded nowhere else. The genealogist who overlooks newspapers misses a great mass of potentially valuable material.*
>
> JAMES L. HANSEN, CG, FASG
> "Research in Newspapers"
> In *The Source: A Guidebook of American Genealogy*

While records of birth, marriage, and death are the most commonly sought and the most consistently helpful records, only the genealogist's imagination and resourcefulness limit newspapers' usefulness in supplying clues about historical events, local history, probate court and legal notices, real estate transactions, political biographies, announcements, notices of new and terminated partnerships, business advertisements, and notices for settling debts.

CAPTAIN DYER SINKING.

Twelfth Precinct Officer's Condition Is a
Subject of Grave Apprehension
to His Family.

A serious change has taken place in the
condition of Captain Edwin Brough Dyer, the
commanding officer of the Twelfth Precinct
station on Atlantic and Schenectady avenues,
and it is believed by the intimate friends of
the sick man that he is rapidly nearing
death. Captain Dyer has been on the sick
list since the day after the last election,
but at no time since then has his condition
been so alarming as it is to-day. The captain is suffering from liver complaint and
his case has for a long time puzzled his

CAPTAIN EDWIN B. DYER,
Who Is Dangerously Ill at His Home.

Newspapers can provide at least a partial substitute for nonexistent civil records. For example, a person's obituary may have appeared in a newspaper even when civil death records for that person do not exist. And newspapers are an important source of marriage records, particularly in those states where civil recording of marriages was essentially nonexistent until the twentieth century.

Unlike official records, newspapers are not limited to a particular geographical area. They often include reports of the weddings of local citizens (even those that occurred in a neighboring county or another state), and they sometimes report visits of geographically distant relatives or the visits of former local residents. They often published death notices of individuals who had left the area long before but who still had local family or friends as well. In each case the newspaper account can identify the date and place of an event, thus opening the possibility of turning up additional documentation in other sources.

The first step in searching a newspaper is to identify those which served the area of interest and which have survived. The three most necessary tools are bibliographies (What was published?), inventories of library and depository holdings (Where is it?), and indexes (How do I find what I want in it?).

OBITUARIES

An "obit" may be the only record of death that you find, especially since civil death registration did not begin until the 1900s. An obit may include the name, age, and birth date of the deceased; parents' names; maiden name, if female; where died; date of death; cause of death; name of spouse and children or survivors; religious affiliation (or allusion to church where married or providing funeral services, or the cemetery of interment); place of burial, if any (there won't be any if, for example, the person was cremated or died in war or at sea); whether the body will be transported to another area or state for burial; military service (or allusion to membership in veterans' group or group honor guard); occupation or name of employer; club or fraternal memberships.

LINDA HERRICK SWISHER
In *Ancestry* magazine

Most obituaries do not include as much data as Linda Swisher mentioned, and for some people, no obituary is ever published. While an obituary can provide many genealogical clues, it is the deceased who possessed the most accurate details; whoever provided details to the newspaper may have given incorrect data (or the newspaper may have printed it incorrectly). Because newspapers are secondary sources, corroborate your findings with other sources, if possible.

Necrologies may be published in local newspapers near the end of a year. These list people who died in the town or area during the year. I know of one newspaper that published a list of members of the county's Early Settler's Association who had died during the year. The lists typically provide the age, name of the deceased's spouse, place of residence, and the year the deceased first came to the county. A necrology may list people who were interred in a cemetery that no longer exists and has no known records.

Chapter 12, "Research in Newspapers," by James L. Hansen, in *The Source: A Guidebook of American Genealogy* includes outstanding detail about what can be found in old newspapers and how to use this valuable source most efficiently.

LAND RECORDS

Most land records will be found with the county recorder's office, the registrar's office, or in the county court at the county seat. Despite their titles, deeds found in a county recorder's office may include other legal documents of transfer, such as deeds in fee simple granting absolute ownership; mortgages transferring property rights as security for debts; dower releases waiving wives' rights; quit-claim deeds releasing whatever title or right is held whether valid or not; deeds of gift transferring land without reciprocal consideration; powers of attorney appointing legal agents; marriage property settlements; bills of sale transferring property that is usually not land; and various forms of contracts, such as leases, partnerships, indenture papers, and other performance bonds. Deed books from before the Civil War and especially in colonial years were more miscellaneous in their contents, even including animal brands, occasional wills, slave manumissions, apprentice papers, petitions, depositions, tax lists, and whatever else the clerk decided to preserve on a convenient page. Through such records a researcher may trace the ownership of land, in some cases for two centuries or more. See more on land records in chapter 3, "Federal Records."

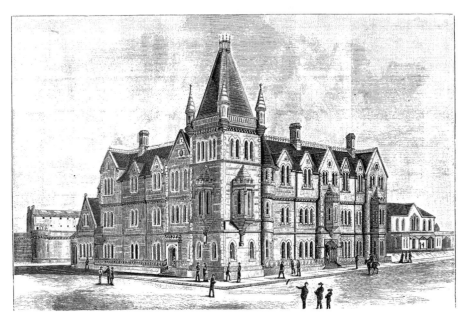

HISTORICAL SOCIETIES AND MUSEUMS

Museums, even those that seem to specialize in rather narrow interests, have a wide range of material; patrons often donate things unrelated to the original collection, and these are usually stored, not discarded or passed on somewhere else. Do not take it for granted that a museum specializing in railroad history may not have a record of frontier scouts, or a historic jail may not have the log books for a local grain mill.

> *The key is always to see the human side of history and look for the personal records your ancestors left within the community record. The individuals you meet today are the custodians of that history and your best guide to the genealogy within it.*
>
> ANNE ROSS BALHUIZEN
> In *Searching on Location: Planning a Research Trip*

Local histories, family histories, biographical collections, historical and genealogical periodicals, published local records, city directories, vital records, school records, military rosters, newspapers, obituaries, yearbooks, scrapbooks, photograph collections, indexes of all sorts, and records that can't be found anywhere else: these are the treasures of historical societies. From those such as the State Historical Society of Wisconsin, which may be the largest, to a tiny room in the basement of a library, historical societies are incredible sources for personal history. Cities, towns, professional groups, religious groups, ethnic groups, and other groups seeking to preserve their history may have saved items or documents that concern your family members. *The Ancestry Family Historian's Address Book* lists genealogical and historical societies, libraries, museums, and archives, as well as federal, state, regional, and local agencies whose collections include materials useful for genealogical and historical research. For each organization the address book lists street address, mailing address, telephone number, fax number, e-mail, and Internet address (where applicable).

Selected Reading

Balhuizen, Anne Ross. *Searching on Location: Planning a Research Trip.* Salt Lake City: Ancestry, 1992.

Frisch-Ripley, Karen. *Unlocking the Secrets in Old Photographs.* Salt Lake City: Ancestry, 1991.

Greenwood, Val D. *Researcher's Guide to American Genealogy.* 2nd ed. Baltimore: Genealogical Publishing Co., 1990.

Kemp, Thomas Jay. *International Vital Records Handbook.* 3rd ed. Baltimore: Genealogical Publishing Co., 1994

Smith, Juliana Szucs. *The Ancestry Family Historian's Address Book: A Comprehensive List of Local, State, and Federal Agencies and Institutions and Ethnic and Genealogical Organizations.* Salt Lake City: Ancestry, 1998.

Szucs, Loretto Dennis, and Sandra Hargreaves Luebking, eds. *The Source: A Guidebook of American Genealogy.* Rev. ed. Salt Lake City: Ancestry, 1997.

Chapter Five

State Records

Many researchers need not leave their own states to obtain documentation [for their family history]. ... Although procedures vary, it is possible to make some generalizations that may ease the way for first-time visitors to a state archives or historical society. Registration is universally required, accompanied by the furnishing of a set of rules and a descriptive pamphlet or leaflet describing the services of the facility. ...Generally there is no charge for access to state records, except for the user fees required by some societies. Reference staff at state archives usually respond to written or telephoned inquiries if they refer to only one or two specific matters that can be answered with a minimum of effort and time.

JAMES C. NEAGLES
In *U.S. Military Records: A Guide to Federal and State Sources, Colonial America to the Present*

Every state in the United States has unique records reflecting the history of individuals and the state as a whole. State archives, historical and genealogical societies, and major research libraries are the primary state organizations that hold relevant records. Generally, there is no charge for access to state records except for mail and photocopy fees where they apply.

As a rule, archivists and librarians at state facilities will respond to reasonable requests so long as they do not require more than a few minutes of research time. Usually, limited staffing makes staff research impossible, and researchers are urged to visit in person or to employ a professional local researcher. Names and addresses of local researchers are often available from these organizations.

GUIDES TO STATE ARCHIVES AND HISTORICAL AGENCIES

It is wise to acquaint yourself with any repository which you might visit by writing to the appropriate archive or library in advance. Every repository has published materials that introduce its collections and research policy. State archives and historical agencies also have Internet sites that provide the same information. Some even have downloadable databases for some or parts of their collections.

Almost every state archive or historical agency has a published catalog of its holdings. An example is *A Summary Guide to Local Governmental Records in the Illinois Regional Archives*. It is a guide to the archival records of local governmental agencies which the Illinois State Archives houses and administers at seven regional depositories on university campuses throughout the state. The guide lists holdings by county and by title. A similar work is *Guide to Records in the New York State Archives*. The introduction to this guide notes that "The New York State Archives and Records Administration (SARA), part of the Office of Cultural Education in the State Education Department, is the organization responsible for identifying, preserving, and making available the permanently valuable records of State government." The holdings of the New York State Archives comprise a unique resource documenting colonial and state government from Dutch settlement in the 1630s to recent years.

STATEWIDE REFERENCE BOOKS

The State Historical Society of Missouri in Columbia holds the most complete newspaper collection. The earliest extant is the Missouri Gazette, 1808–14, *which has been microfilmed. The society has published* Guide to Missouri Newspapers: When and Where 1808–1963.

MARSHA HOFFMAN RISING, CG, FASG
"Missouri"
In *Ancestry's Red Book: American State, County and Town Sources*

Before visiting or writing state offices, it is helpful to have some idea of how records will be cataloged or found. American county boundaries have changed over the years, and without precise information on how historical events have altered county lines, you might waste precious time. In addition to maps for every state that clearly outline every county, *Ancestry's Red Book* provides a key to county locations on each state map; county government address; date the county was formed and parent counties; when birth, marriage, and death registrations began in the county; and when land,

probate, and court records began for the county. Additionally, each state section provides a brief history of the state's settlement patterns; a history and unique aspects of each state's vital record keeping; extant state, federal, and special censuses; special maps for the state; a description of land records (including unusual ones) in the state; special features about probate, court, tax, cemetery, church, military, and naturalization records; and special ethnic, newspaper, and manuscript collections in each state.

State census records are among the more unique records to be found at the state level. In *State Census Records*, Ann S. Lainhart notes that "State censuses may fill in gaps left by missing federal censuses. State censuses may not be closed to the public for a seventy-two-year period as are federal censuses; in fact some state censuses taken as recently as 1945 are available to the public."

GENEALOGICAL GUIDES TO SPECIFIC STATES

For a few states there are specific genealogical guides, and more of these are being published all the time. You can keep up with new publications by reading genealogical magazines, journals, newsletters, and catalogs from genealogical vendors. The Internet is also an excellent vehicle for discovering what is available for individual states. Among published state guides, the following are good examples:

Roseann Hogan's *Kentucky Ancestry: A Guide to Genealogical and Historical Research* outlines the holdings of the commonwealth's major statewide archives and libraries, along with information on courthouses, local libraries, and regional historical societies for each of Kentucky's 120 counties. Kip Sperry's *Genealogical Research in Ohio* is designed for quick reference and bibliographic completeness. It discusses various record sources, such as military, marriage, and tax records, and cites published works and microfilmed collections to aid the researcher.

The Minnesota Historical Society's *Genealogical Resources of the Minnesota Historical Society: A Guide* is a wonderful example of a state government production. It was compiled for the numerous genealogists who have already used the resources of the Minnesota Historical Society for documenting family and local history, and for other historians who want to identify resources for topics of new social history. While not a complete inventory of all resources, this work serves as a guide to many of them and introduces even the most experienced researchers to new areas for exploration. It is arranged alphabetically, with annotated listings of resources by name of subject area. The entry for each resource describes content, location, and means of access. Bette Marie Barker's *Guide to Family History Sources in the New Jersey State Archives* is a similar compilation. This guide provides an overview of state and federal census records, vital records, county marriages, marriage bonds, newspapers, tax ratables, military records, naturalizations, wills and probate records, deeds, court records, and other county records together with date spans (1625 to 1925 for some).

SELECTED READING

Bailey, Robert E., and Elaine Shemoney Evans, et al., eds. *A Summary Guide to Local Governmental Records in the Illinois Regional Archives.* Springfield: Office of the Secretary of State, Illinois State Archives, 1992.

Barker, Bette Marie, Daniel P. Jones, and Karl J. Niederer, comps. *Guide to Family History Sources in the New Jersey State Archives.* Trenton: New Jersey Department of State, Division of Archives and Records Management, 1990.

Eichholz, Alice, ed. *Ancestry's Red Book: American State, County and Town Sources.* Rev. ed. Salt Lake City: Ancestry, 1992.

Hogan, Roseann Reinmuth *Kentucky Ancestry: A Guide to Genealogical and Historical Research.* Salt Lake City: Ancestry, 1992.

Lainhart, Ann S. *State Census Records.* Baltimore: Genealogical Publishing Co., 1992.

Minnesota Historical Society, Library and Archives Division. *Genealogical Resources of the Minnesota Historical Society: A Guide.* 2nd ed. St. Paul: Minnesota Historical Society Press, 1993.

Neagles, James C. *U.S. Military Records: A Guide to Federal and State Sources, Colonial America to the Present.* Salt Lake City: Ancestry, 1994.

Smith, Juliana Szucs. *The Ancestry Family Historian's Address Book: A Comprehensive List of Local, State, and Federal Agencies and Institutions and Ethnic and Genealogical Organizations.* Salt Lake City: Ancestry, 1998.

State Archives and Records Administration. *Guide to Records in the New York State Archives.* Albany, N.Y.: State Archives and Records Administration, State Education Department, The University of the State of New York, 1993.

Sperry, Kip. *Genealogical Research in Ohio*. Baltimore: Genealogical
Publishing Co., 1997.

Chapter Six

$\mathcal{G}$ENEALOGICAL $\mathcal{S}$OCIETIES

*Genealogists are generally positive and energetic, and most are
ready to share their findings or research experience with anyone they can help. There are hundreds of genealogical societies
at the grass-roots level. Knowledge of the genealogical community will place you in the midst of much activity, increase
your productivity, and alert you to the importance of research
standards and etiquette.*

SANDRA HARGREAVES LUEBKING
Editor of the Federation of Genealogical Societies *Forum*
Co-editor of *The Source: A Guidebook of American Genealogy*

$\mathcal{B}$ecause family history research relies greatly upon records
found at the county level, many local societies represent
counties. Organizations also form around shared interests.
Ethnic or religious origins account for many groups, such as the
Polish Genealogical Society of America and P.O.I.N.T.
(Pursuing Our Italian Names Together). Societies also form
around common locales of origin for members' ancestors;
hence, the Palatines to America and Germans from Russia societies. To locate these and other societies, consult Juliana Szucs
Smith's *The Ancestry Family Historian's Address Book*. It lists
addresses, telephone and fax numbers, and Internet addresses of
thousands of organizations throughout the United States.

For almost every state there is a state genealogical society, a state genealogical council, or both. In addition to their own work, state-level groups sometimes help coordinate the efforts of local societies within the state. Their publications, newsletters and quarterlies, supplement those produced by the local societies.

GENEALOGICAL SOCIETIES AT THE NATIONAL LEVEL

At the national level, a number of organizations seek to serve individual genealogists or societies. The Federation of Genealogical Societies (FGS) is an umbrella organization for local, state, and other organizations, such as genealogical societies, libraries, archives, and institutes. The National Genealogical Society (NGS) is comprised of individual researchers. The oldest society is the New England Historic Genealogical Society in Boston.

Founded in 1976, the FGS is a nonprofit organization composed of nearly five hundred genealogical and historical societies, family associations, and libraries, ultimately representing nearly 200,000 individual genealogists. The federation is the collective voice of organizations at the national level. It is actively involved in representing societies, coordinating and facilitating their activities, and monitoring events that are critical to the future of genealogy.

Among the major projects in which the Federation has taken the leading role is the Civil War Soldiers and Sailors System (CWSS), a computerized database containing basic facts about servicemen who served on both sides during the Civil War; a list of regiments in both the Union and Confederate armies; identification and descriptions of 384 significant battles of the war; references that identify sources of the information in the database; and suggestions for finding additional information. The CWSS is made possible by partnerships with the National Park Service, the National Archives, the Family History Library, and several other organizations. (See chapter 10, "Family History, Computers, and the Internet.")

Most genealogical societies undertake valuable indexing and preservation activities and produce newsletters, journals, and other publications that benefit the genealogical community. Societies also provide educational opportunities for members and nonmembers in their areas. These can range from sponsoring adult education courses to hosting seminars with nationally known lecturers. Almost every genealogical society produces a newsletter or holds a meeting on a monthly basis. These meetings offer opportunities for beginners and experienced family historians to meet, exchange ideas, stay current on important issues that affect genealogical research, and hear local record keepers and experts address timely and relevant topics.

The FGS Membership Directory is a tremendous resource that can be used to identify many of the hard-to-find publications produced by genealogical and historical societies as well as information on how to join a local society in an area of geographic interest.

DAVID E. RENCHER, AG, FUGA
President, Federation of Genealogical Societies

FGS Society Hall on Ancestry's World Wide Web site (http://www.ancestry.com) provides complete information for each FGS member genealogical society, including

    Name and address of the genealogical society
    Telephone number
    E-mail address
    Web site URL (if applicable)
    Contact person
    Number of members
    Description of periodicals, publications, and services

Genealogical societies that are not members of FGS are listed with addresses, telephone numbers, and e-mail and URL addresses only.

For more than 150 years, historians and genealogical societies have been printing periodicals (serials, journals, and magazines) that include a large variety of original sources, abstracts, transcripts, how-to articles, and compiled family histories that represent a vast resource for family historians. These hard-to-find articles have been indexed in the Allen County (Indiana) Public Library's *Periodical Source Index* (*PERSI*), a comprehensive index that includes more than a million detailed entries from a vast variety of genealogical articles in over five thousand periodicals. This index is available in book, microfiche, and CD-ROM formats. While previously it was necessary to search every category in each of the twenty-nine printed volumes, the CD-ROM version (Ancestry, 1998) enables you to instantly scan the entire database, identify and print out details about articles of interest, including publisher, magazine or journal publishing date, and information about ordering copies of the articles.

GENEALOGICAL CONFERENCES
National genealogical conferences, sponsored by national, local, and ethnic groups, are held annually in different parts of the United States. Genealogical societies usually advertise these important events in their own publications, and they also distribute information about upcoming conferences to libraries, archives, and other places where family historians tend to congregate.

National Genealogical Society
4527 Seventeenth Street North
Arlington, VA 22207-2399
http://www.genealogy.org/~ngs/

The Federation of Genealogical Societies
P.O. Box 830220
Richardson, TX 75083-0220
http://www.fgs.org.

An award-winning home study course titled "American Genealogy: A Basic Course" is offered by the National Genealogical Society, Education Department, at the address listed above.

SELECTED READING

Smith, Juliana Szucs. *The Ancestry Family Historian's Address Book: A Comprehensive List of Local, State, and Federal Agencies and Institutions and Ethnic and Genealogical Organizations.* Salt Lake City: Ancestry, 1998.

PERiodical Source Index (PERSI) ver. 2.0. CD-ROM. Salt Lake City: Ancestry, 1998.

Chapter Seven

$\mathcal{F}$OREIGN, $\mathcal{E}$THNIC, AND $\mathcal{R}$ELIGIOUS $\mathcal{R}$ESEARCH

*One of the beautiful ironies of modern American history was
that the children of refugees from the Old World had the
wealth, the leisure, and the technical means to return for a holiday to the scenes of their parents' poverty and oppression. The
man whose ancestor had fled penniless and in desperation from
Sicily or Ireland or Germany returned in air conditioned com-
fort to rediscover the "romance" of the Old World.*

DANIEL J. BOORSTIN
In *The Americans: The Democratic Experience*

ETHNIC RESEARCH

North America has always been a land of ethnic diversity. Each of
us has been touched in some way by the experiences, choices, attitudes, and even the genetic makeup of our ethnic ancestors. Those
who have gone before us have had a profound influence in shap-
ing our world.

Every ethnic group had its own kinds of records and record-
keeping systems. While records of religious events in individuals'

lives may be the primary source of biographical information for members of one ethnic group, the foreign-language press, an ethnic benevolent society, an immigrant insurance program, or a fraternal organization might be the best source for members of another. Knowledge of an ancestor's ethnic group, its history, settlement patterns, and its laws and customs can lead us to specific and often unique record sources. Such background knowledge puts you in a better position to interpret whatever you may find in the records you use.

More importantly, ethnic sources can help us to understand our ancestors as real people. Without cultural background information, we are often at a loss to understand their actions. But with some comprehension of the group of which they were a part, and the times in which they lived, we can begin to understand them more clearly. More than lifeless names on family charts, we begin to see our ancestors as human beings with distinct personalities.

It is a common misconception to think of "ethnic" as referring to someone or something foreign; yet most dictionaries

define the word as of or relating to large groups of people, classed according to common racial, national, tribal, religious, linguistic, or cultural origin or background. By this definition, it would seem that all family history studies are ethnic.

One of the most definitive and useful background sources for almost every ethnic group is Stephan Thurstrom's *Harvard Encyclopedia of American Ethnic Groups*. This work contains basic information about the multitude of people who make up the population of the United States. It is a succinct, authoritative synthesis of the origins and histories of 106 ethnic groups with twenty-nine thematic essays, eighty-seven maps, and a critical bibliography for each section.

Few of those whose ancestors arrived on the Mayflower would think of their families as "ethnic" in any way. However, if we adhere to the definition of the word, we have to concede that the English pioneers were as ethnic as the Native Americans who were their predecessors in North America. There are distinct skills and bodies of ethnic records that a Mayflower descendant needs to know in order to be fully effective in conducting research. *Plymouth Colony: Its History and People, 1620–1691* by Eugene Stratton, for example, provides an account of the history and genealogy of Plymouth Colony. This well-documented source includes a history of the colony, both chronologically and topically, and biographical sketches of more than three hundred of its inhabitants.

Alice Eichholz's *Ancestry's Red Book: American State, County and Town Sources* is an expansive guide to useful resources in the United States. For each state there is a brief historical background discussion, including settlement patterns, that will provide helpful background information for ethnic research. For each state a section titled "Special Focus Category" describes ethnic sources unique to the particular state.

The Oklahoma chapter in the *Red Book*, for example, provides a lengthy narrative of Native American collections and a surprisingly large bibliography of Oklahoma Native American source materials. A separate bibliography cites volumes that analyze the role and impact of other major ethnic groups in the state. For example, the Oklahoma chapter identifies a series of books about African Americans, British, Irish, Czechs, Italians, Germans, Germans from Russia, Mexicans, Jews, and Poles in Oklahoma.

Under the *Red Book*'s section on Pennsylvania you will find such references as John E. Bodner's *Ethnic History of Pennsylvania: A Selected Bibliography*. Also useful is David E.

Washburn's *The Peoples of Pennsylvania: An Annotated Bibliography of Resource Materials.*

After you've completed ethnic research on this side of the ocean, move on to guides designed specifically for helping you to discover records about your family in your immigrant ancestor's homeland. The challenges of tracing Irish ancestors back to their homeland, for example, are complex and sometimes frustrating. Dr. James G. Ryan has compiled a comprehensive work that provides a county-by-county list of record sources in Ireland along with a discussion of how to use them. Ryan's book, *Irish Records: Sources for Family and Local History,* provides short histories and record inventories and describes research facilities and services for each of Ireland's thirty-two counties.

Italian Genealogical Records: How to Use Italian Civil, Ecclesiastical, and Other Records in Family History Research by Trafford R. Cole is the counterpart of Ryan's book if you have Italian ancestry. In it, Cole describes how to use documents that record the histories of Italian families. If you claim German origins, you will want to consult Kevan M. Hansen's *Your German Ancestry: A Genealogist and Historian's Guide to Research in Germany.* This brief guide is an up-to-date source book for German research, including information on accessing German archives on the Internet.

Judith Prowse Reid's *Genealogical Research in England's Public Record Office: A Guide for North Americans* is an award-winning guide to records that are critical to many American research projects. Reid notes that the Public Record Office (PRO) in London is one of the world's great repositories of original source documents. The international collections of the PRO (which is the English equivalent to the National Archives in Canada and the United States) include records of government and law courts from the *Domesday Book* of 1086 to the present.

Sherry Irvine has compiled two acclaimed guides for British research. *Your English Ancestry: A Guide for North Americans* and

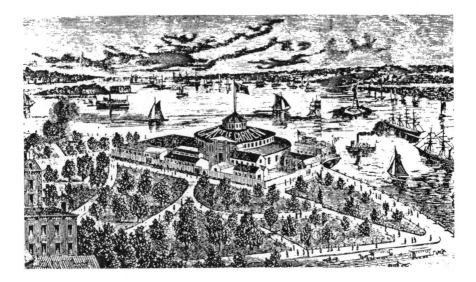

Your Scottish Ancestry: A Guide for North Americans present clear instructions for using the many records described. Strategic planning concepts presented in both of Irvine's guides enable the researcher to make the best use of English and Scottish records dating back to the 1600s without leaving North America.

Through the Internet you can find information on virtually every ethnic group and countless opportunities to expand your knowledge. Large and small ethnic, genealogical, and historical organizations have posted World Wide Web pages with a variety of useful information, databases, maps, and photographs.

RELIGIOUS RECORDS

Church records rank among the most promising of genealogical records available. Indeed, for periods before the advent of civil registration of vital statistics (a very late development in many American states), church records rank as the best available sources for information on specific vital events: birth, marriage, and death.

They are also among the most under-used major records in American genealogy. Part of the reason lies in the number of denominations—there are hundreds of them. Identifying and locating the records of these various churches makes even professional genealogists hesitate. Yet the task is not impossible. Microfilming, photocopying, and indexing techniques make church records more accessible now than ever before.

RICHARD W. DOUGHERTY, AUTHOR
"Research in Church Records"
In *The Source: A Guidebook of American Genealogy*

*To be descended from a famous rabbi is considered a mark of honor, and famous rabbis have documented their pedigrees (*yichus *in Hebrew) to show their Jewish "blue blood."*

GARY MOKOTOFF
"Tracking Jewish-American Family History"
In *The Source: A Guidebook of American Genealogy*

Traditionally, different denominations have kept different types of records. For example, presbyteries transferred membership records with the departure of a member. Catholics and Lutherans carefully record baptisms and infant births. Names of godparents may be the most needed clues to be found in records, since close relatives were often chosen to assume responsibility for infants should anything happen to their parents. In contrast, Baptist records contain more important information about adult members because Baptists are baptized later in life.

Baptisms recorded in church ledgers almost always list the name of the person baptized, the names of his or her parents, the date and place of birth, and the date of the baptism. Most

denominations have recorded marriages, and these usually predate civil
registration; however, they vary widely
in content, some providing nothing
more than the names of the bride and
groom and the date of the event. Yet,
in others, the inclusion of witnesses'
names will provide critical clues to
continued research (witnesses were
often related or belonged to the same
social circle). Death and burial records
also vary from one denomination to another. While one register will provide the name and date of death only, others may
provide birth dates and even birthplaces. This information can
be especially useful in cases where the birthplace is an unknown
foreign place. Records kept by one denomination can also vary
from one ethnic group to another. German Catholics, for example, were meticulous record-keepers who were more likely to
keep track of details.

Immigrants commonly chose to worship in their native
tongue, so they often went far from home to find the congenial
atmosphere of the house of worship of fellow countrymen.
Churches as well as people responded to the dynamics of
cities—some closing, consolidating, or moving as neighborhoods changed, others shifting from their ethnic orientation to
accommodate new circumstances. Thus, if you have difficulty
finding religious records you might save time by backtracking
to study the history of religions in the locale of interest.

In addition to baptism, marriage, and burial records, there are
some other church records worth searching for. Confirmation
records are often no more than lists of names, but some
Scandinavian American Lutheran confirmation records contain
significant biographical detail. Membership rosters, church census records, historical commemorative publications, and religious newspapers can also be sources of vital information.

Religious newspapers often contain biographical sketches and obituaries found nowhere else.

Though religious records can be more difficult to find than others, the time and effort required is usually well spent. These collections often supply information not found elsewhere—sometimes indicating even former residences. And sometimes that former residence will mean the discovery of the name of the town or church of origin in the "Old Country."

Relatively few church or other religious records have been published, so it is usually necessary to locate the original records. *The National Directory of Churches, Synagogues, and Other Houses of Worship,* edited by John Kroll, attempts to list the name, address, and telephone number of every active house of worship in the United States. Each volume covers a distinct geographic area. Juliana Szucs Smith's *The Ancestry Family Historian's Address Book* lists some church archives.

Many churches of all denominations have closed over the years, and many that remain no longer have sufficient space or staff to conduct research, so the records have become less accessible. Older records of almost all denominations are sometimes more easily found and accessed through the Family History Library than more recent records. Millions of records of religious events from churches of all kinds and in almost every country have been preserved on microfilm and are now available at and through the Family History Library. (See chapter 8, "The Family History Library and Its Centers.")

For the millions who need to find Catholic relatives' church records, *U.S. Catholic Sources: A Diocesan Research Guide* by Virginia Humling is an invaluable help. While the parish is the most fundamental unit for researching Roman Catholic records, diocesan archives often contain copies of diocesan newspapers and records from closed parishes. For every archdiocese and diocese in the united States, this guide identifies the records available at each location.

The Encyclopedia of Jewish Genealogy: Sources in the United States and Canada, edited by Arthur Kurzweil and Miriam Weiner, provides a unique view of the diversity of research possibilities and resources that are available. *The Sourcebook for Jewish Genealogy and Family Histories* by David Zubatsky and Irwin M. Berent is the most comprehensive bibliography of published and unpublished family histories and individual family names compiled from books, newspaper and journal articles, Jewish encyclopedia entries, family papers, and family trees. In "Tracking Jewish American Family History" in *The Source: A Guidebook of American Genealogy*, Gary Mokotoff offers a survey of the history of Jewish migration, first outlining the movements of Jews throughout the world during the full course of their history, and then describing six phases of Jewish immigration to the United States in more detail. The author makes an important point, observing that each of these periods "has its own sources of information for doing genealogical research."

SELECTED READING

Bodner, John E. *Ethnic History of Pennsylvania: A Selected Bibliography.* Harrisburg: Pennsylvania Historical Museum Commission, 1974.

Boorstin, Daniel J. *The Americans: The Democratic Experience.* New York: Random House, 1973.

Cole, Trafford R. *Italian Genealogical Records: How to Use Italian Civil, Ecclesiastical, and Other Records in Family History Research.* Salt Lake City: Ancestry, 1995.

Eichholz, Alice, ed. *Ancestry's Red Book: American State, County and Town Sources.* Rev. ed. Salt Lake City: Ancestry, 1992.

Hansen, Kevan M. *Your German Ancestry: A Genealogist and Historian's Guide to Research in Germany.* Salt Lake City: Ancestry, 1998.

Harris, Maurine and Glen. *Ancestry's Concise Genealogical Dictionary.* Salt Lake City: Ancestry, 1989.

Hogan, Roseann Reinemuth. *Kentucky Ancestry: A Guide to Genealogical and Historical Research.* Salt Lake City: Ancestry, 1992.

Humling, Virginia. *U.S. Catholic Sources: A Diocesan Guide.* Salt Lake City: Ancestry, 1995.

Irvine, Sherry. *Your English Ancestry: A Guide for North Americans.* Salt Lake City: Ancestry, 1993.

—————. *Your Scottish Ancestry: A Guide for North Americans.* Salt Lake City: Ancestry, 1997.

Kroll, John, ed. *The National Directory of Churches, Synagogues, and Other Houses of Worship.* Detroit: Gale Research, 1994.

Kurzweil, Arthur, and Miriam Weiner. *The Encyclopedia of Jewish Genealogy: Sources in the United States and Canada.* Northvale, N.J.: Jason Aronson, 1991.

Meyerink, Kory L., ed. *Printed Sources: A Guide to Published Genealogical Records.* Salt Lake City: Ancestry, 1998.

Mills, Elizabeth Shown. *Evidence! Citation and Analysis for the Family Historian.* Baltimore: Genealogical Publishing Co., 1997.

Reid, Judith Prowse. *Genealogical Research in England's Public Record Office: A Guide for North Americans.* Baltimore: Genealogical Publishing Co., 1996.

Ryan, James G. *Irish Records: Sources for Family and Local History.* Rev. ed. Salt Lake City: Ancestry, 1997.

Smith, Juliana Szucs. *The Ancestry Family Historian's Address Book: A Comprehensive List of Local, State, and Federal Agencies and Institutions and Ethnic and Genealogical Organizations.* Salt Lake City: Ancestry, 1998.

Stratton, Eugene. *Plymouth Colony: Its History and People, 1620–1691.* Salt Lake City: Ancestry, 1986.

Szucs, Loretto Dennis. *Chicago and Cook County: A Guide to Research:* Salt Lake City: Ancestry, 1996.

Szucs, Loretto Dennis, and Sandra Hargreaves Luebking, eds. *The Source: A Guidebook of American Genealogy.* Rev. ed. Salt Lake City: Ancestry, 1997.

Thurstrom, Stephan. *Harvard Encyclopedia of American Ethnic Groups.* Cambridge, Mass.: The Belknap Press of Harvard University Press, 1980.

Washburn, David E., comp. and ed. *The Peoples of Pennsylvania: An Annotated Bibliography of Resource Materials.* Pittsburgh, Pa.: University of International Studies, University of Pittsburgh, 1981.

Zubatsky, David, and Irwin M. Berent. *The Sourcebook for Jewish Genealogy and Family Histories.* Teaneck, N.J.: Avotaynu, 1996.

Chapter Eight

$\mathcal{T}$HE $\mathcal{F}$AMILY $\mathcal{H}$ISTORY $\mathcal{L}$IBRARY AND $\mathcal{I}$TS $\mathcal{C}$ENTERS

The Family History Library is the largest library in the world specializing in collecting genealogical or family history material. Sometimes called the "mecca" of genealogy, the Family History Library attracts many family historians who plan trips and vacation time to come to Salt Lake City, Utah, to use the worldwide collections housed in the library's five-story building.

KORY L. MEYERINK
In *The Source: A Guidebook of American Genealogy*

$\mathcal{T}$he scope of the Family History Library's collections, as well as the easy access provided by its thousands of branch libraries, make it an outstanding resource for every family historian. The library's history dates back to 1894, when the Genealogical Society of Utah was founded to gather and preserve the various records that help people trace their ancestry. Shortly after its founding, the society opened a library which later became the Family History Library. In 1938 the society began preserving records on microfilm, and it continues to microfilm birth, marriage, death, probate, immigration, military, and many other records in more than fifty countries. Through this program, the library has acquired the world's largest collection of genealogical information. Since 1944 the library (as well as the Genealogical Society of Utah) has been wholly owned and operated by The Church of Jesus Christ of Latter-day Saints (also known as the LDS church). While the library is maintained as a resource for LDS church members, anyone, regardless of race, creed, or religion, is welcome to visit the library and use its collections and services at no charge. In 1964 a system of branch libraries, now called family history centers, was established to give more people access to the library's resources.

MICROFILM COLLECTIONS
The library's collection includes approximately 2 million rolls of microfilmed records and more than 500,000 microfiche. These records were created by governments, churches of many denominations, other organizations, and individuals. The library also has copies of church registers, census records, passenger lists, military records, land records, and probate records. Most of the records date from around 1550 to about 1920. The library has collected records for many areas of the world, particularly the countries in which many North Americans have roots.

North America
The Family History Library's largest collection covers the United States. More than half a million microfilm rolls represent every state. At least 100,000 of those rolls contain federal records (including census, military, and immigration records). These records are from more than 2,300 archives, county courthouses, and other repositories, the majority from the states east of the Mississippi River. There are at least thirty-five thousand rolls for Canada, and almost all Quebec church records and

many civil records from Ontario and other provinces are included.

British Areas

The more than 155,000 microfilm rolls for Great Britain include a comprehensive collection of Scottish records, as well as a very large collection of records from England. The library also has significant collections for Ireland and Wales, with many records also available for Australia and New Zealand.

Europe

The European microfilms form the second-largest collection at the library; there are more than half a million rolls. They include church and civil records for many areas of Germany and France (more than 100,000 rolls each). Virtually all major genealogical records are available for the Netherlands (ninety thousand rolls), Belgium (sixty-six thousand rolls), Hungary (twelve thousand rolls), and Luxembourg. The fastest growth in the European collections is for the countries of Italy, Poland, Portugal, Spain, and Switzerland.

Scandinavia

The library's collection of more than 200,000 microfilms for Denmark (ninety-five thousand rolls), Sweden (seventy-nine thousand rolls), Norway (twelve thousand rolls), and Finland (fifteen thousand rolls) provides virtually comprehensive coverage for these countries.

Latin America

Most church parish records are included in the collections for Mexico (140,000 rolls), Chile (eight thousand rolls), and Uruguay. Another fifty thousand rolls provide growing, but still incomplete, coverage for the other Latin countries, most notably Argentina, Brazil, and Guatemala (each with at least eight thousand rolls).

Other Areas
Other countries for which the library has comprehensive collections include the Philippines (fifty-one thousand rolls), Sri Lanka, many Pacific islands, and many smaller countries. There are partial collections for South Africa and many other countries. The library has a growing collection of family histories for China, Japan, and Korea.

BOOK AND OTHER COLLECTIONS

The library has more than a quarter of a million books, including published family histories, local histories, indexes, periodicals, and other research aids. More than half of this collection is also available on microfilm or microfiche. Many thousands of the library's microfilms are reproductions of books that are not available (in book form) at the library. Many of these are obscure books not easily found in other libraries and which may have been out of print for decades.

The library also has a very useful collection of maps to help place ancestors in geographic perspective and to aid the research process. Several hundred manuscript pedigrees represent the research of previous family historians. Microfilm copies of most of these are also available.

The library's Automated Resource Center houses electronic materials the library has collected and also provides access to the major online services, such as CompuServe and America Online. The collection of CD-ROMs represents virtually every title available that pertains to local or family history.

FAMILYSEARCH

FamilySearch® is a computerized collection of genealogical information created by the LDS church. It is available through the Family History Library. The collection uses CD-ROM technology to store and retrieve massive amounts of genealogical data. However, it is not available through modem or Internet use as of 1998. The following files and programs are part of FamilySearch:

Ancestral File®
Family History Library Catalog™
International Genealogical Index®
U.S. Social Security Death Index
U.S. Military Index
Scottish Church Records
TempleReady™
Personal Ancestral File®

FAMILY HISTORY LIBRARY CATALOG

The *Family History Library Catalog* is your key to understanding the library's growing collections. It lists and describes each of the microfilms, microfiche, books, compact discs, manuscripts, and all other records in the library. Each year almost 100 million new pages of historical documents are preserved and cataloged (approximately fifty thousand rolls). The catalog is available on CD-ROM and on microfiche; both versions are usually updated annually. Individuals or institutions may purchase the microfiche version of the catalog, or portions of it. With the catalog, you can find records by author, title, subject, locality, or surname. The CD-ROM version of the catalog allows searches by microfilm or microfiche number or by computer number, but not by author, title, or subject.

LIBRARY SERVICES

The library has "open stacks," meaning that patrons can retrieve and use almost all of the materials personally. Copies of most of the microfilms are immediately available in the library and can be used at any of the more than seven hundred microfilm readers and dozens of microfiche readers. Patrons can photocopy selected portions of books, microfilms, and microfiche inexpensively. Copy machines are available on each floor.

Most of the library's microfilms and microfiche can be borrowed through its many family history centers. There is a small postage and duplication fee, and this service can only be requested in person at a local history center (see below).

PREPARING TO VISIT THE LIBRARY

You will be more successful in visiting the library if you are prepared to effectively use its resources. To do this, gather all of the background information you can beforehand, and familiarize yourself with the records you'll need to access in your research. If possible, visit a local family history center before you visit the library. Also note that, while most of the microfilms you'll want to use are kept at the library, some are housed in a different location. If you are planning to use recent (new) films, films of obscure sources, or films for countries outside western Europe and Great Britain, contact the library to check on availability or write to the library at least two weeks in advance and request the films you need.

FAMILY HISTORY CENTERS

The Family History Library currently supports more than 2,500 "branch libraries," called family history centers, throughout the world. As branches of the Family History Library, they can provide access to almost all of the microfilm and microfiche maintained at the main library. Because of the LDS church's interest in genealogical research, these centers have been provided as a way for their members and the entire public to use the resources of the Family History Library (at no charge) without having to travel to Salt Lake City.

Family history centers have been established in most LDS stakes. (A stake is a group of six to twelve "wards," or congregations.) Through them, microfilm and microfiche copies of the records at the Family History Library can be borrowed for a small handling fee. The books at the main library do not circulate, but more than half of them are available on microfilm. Many published sources are under copyright, and in most such cases the Family History Library cannot microfilm them.

Family history centers are found in LDS church buildings throughout the United States and in dozens of foreign countries, generally in or near large population centers. Areas of greater LDS population, such as the western United States, have more family history centers. Usually these centers are about the size of a classroom, and they are equipped with microfilm and microfiche reading machines, computers with the *FamilySearch* program, a copy of the *Family History Library Catalog*, and other major sources, such as *Ancestral File*, the *International Genealogical Index*, and census indexes. The staff are all volunteers with varying experience in genealogical research. You will find them to be quite helpful.

While most centers have a small collection of general reference books, centers do not collect records of the area where they are located. However, because of the size of the Family History Library's collection and the fact that many of the sources are public domain documents and books, most sources that the researcher is seeking are available on microfilm or microfiche and can be sent to any center. Most films are only kept at the centers for a short period of time while patrons use them for their research.

Proselyting is not allowed in family history centers and, on average, more than half of their patrons are not members of the LDS church. For more information on family history centers, see *The Library: A Guide to the LDS Family History Library*.

Some of the older, larger family history centers have collected several thousand books and hundreds of rolls of microfilm. Some of these "regional" libraries are in or near the cities of San Diego, Los Angeles, Oakland, and Sacramento, California; Phoenix, Arizona; Provo and Logan, Utah; Las Vegas, Nevada; Calgary (Alberta), Canada; and Pocatello and Rexburg, Idaho.

The Family History Library is located at 35 North West Temple Street, Salt Lake City, UT 84150 (telephone: 801-240-2331). It is open Monday through Friday from 7:30 a.m. until 10:00 p.m. and on Saturdays from 7:30 a.m. until 5:00 p.m. It is closed on the following holidays each year: New Year's Day, Independence Day, Pioneer Day (a Utah state holiday on or near 24 July), Thanksgiving, Christmas Eve, and Christmas.

The above is based on appendix D, "The Family History Library and Its Centers," by Kory L. Meyerink, in *The Source: A Guidebook of American Genealogy*.

SELECTED READING

Ancestry Reference Library. CD-ROM. Salt Lake City: Ancestry, 1998.

Cerny, Johni, and Wendy Elliott. *The Library: A Guide to the LDS Family History Library.* Salt Lake City: Ancestry, 1988.

Eichholz, Alice, ed. *Ancestry's Red Book: American State, County and Town Sources.* Rev. ed. Salt Lake City: Ancestry, 1992.

Neagles, James C. *The Library of Congress: A Guide to Genealogical and Historical Research.* Salt Lake City: Ancestry, 1990.

———. *U.S. Military Records: A Guide to Federal and State Sources, Colonial America to the Present.* Salt Lake City: Ancestry, 1994.

Parker, Carlyle. *Going to Salt Lake City to Do Family History Research.* 2nd ed. Turlock, Calif.: Marietta Publishing Co., 1993.

Szucs, Loretto Dennis, and Sandra Hargreaves Luebking, eds. *The Archives: A Guide to the National Archives Field Branches.* Salt Lake City: Ancestry, 1988. Also available on CD-ROM as part of Ancestry Reference Library

———, eds. *The Source: A Guidebook of American Genealogy.* Rev. ed. Salt Lake City: Ancestry, 1997.

COLLEGE.IN 1846
Nº 1 COLLEGE 2 INFIRMARY, 3 SEMINARY

Chapter Nine

𝒯HE 𝓗ISTORICAL 𝒟IMENSION

*Family history would be an empty study of names and dates
if it were not possible to flesh out these ghosts of our pasts.
One of the greatest pleasures in genealogy is to learn how
families lived, to understand their experiences including their
ideology, the social milieu, and their physical environment. In
fact, stories of the personal lives and times of our ancestors,
handed down from generation to generation, seem to be the
motivation and inspiration that initially interests many family historians to pursue the quest to know more about these
distant figures.*

ROSEANN REINEMUTH HOGAN
In *Kentucky Ancestry:
A Guide to Genealogical and Historical Research*

*One of the requirements of a good genealogist is a knowledge
of history. He must know about the changing of state and
county lines. A family may have lived a generation in the
same house on the same land and not moved an inch, yet in
thirty years may have resided in three counties and two states.*

The genealogist must know about migration patterns and the trails over which his ancestors moved westward or southward. He must know the ethnic groups that settled in the area of his research, about laws governing probate, immigration and naturalization, and so on.

MILTON RUBINCAM, FASG
In *Pitfalls in Genealogical Research*

History as it was presented to us in school was hardly inviting, and geography, as many of us knew it, simply is not taught anymore in most places. But for the family historian, there is special significance in understanding the history of the nation, province, state, or town where each ancestor lived. To be at least slightly acquainted with the history of a place or a group is almost essential for the success of any research project.

While even an encyclopedia's overview of history might suffice in some instances, you will find that the more you know about a particular place or subject, the better you will be able to recognize clues as they present themselves during your research. It is almost impossible to understand our ancestors' actions if we remove them from the context of their times.

There are plenty of entertaining ways to become familiar with the times and places of our ancestors. If you don't find what you need in your personal library or on the Internet (see chapter 10), your local library is the next logical step. It helps to keep a reading list. Jotting down a book's full title, the author's name, publisher's name, and the publication place and date will save time when you want to refer again to something. As time slips by and the list of sources you've checked grows longer, it may be hard to remember where you found a critical clue. Often, names and events that you read about early in your research will have no meaning, but they may become relevant as you uncover more information.

The newspapers of the time and place where your family lived will provide a fascinating look at the past. Almost every

state has a newspaper project in which old newspapers are collected, microfilmed, and archived. Almost all state libraries and historical agencies have collections of newspapers for all counties that circulate on interlibrary loan.

As noted earlier, local histories often provide an intimate view of events in the places where your ancestors lived. These histories often contain many biographical sketches of prominent citizens. Local histories can usually be found in the libraries in the areas where your ancestors lived. Some libraries have bibliographies that cite books concerning the areas they serve. More recent histories about places, areas, or special events may include photographs that will add an important dimension to your research. Who wouldn't like to see a farm, village, or street as it looked in 1870 when Great-Grandfather walked there?

The more you study the history of times and places, the more you'll understand the reasons for your ancestors' actions and the more you'll know about where to look for further information.

> *For genealogists who complain that historians do not take them seriously, there can be no greater respect than the kind that comes from serious scholarly achievement. Historians will learn, as well, that genealogists have significant contributions to make to their understanding of history.*
>
> RAFAEL GUBER
> In *Ancestry* magazine

MAPS, ATLASES, AND GAZETTEERS

Perhaps the most endearing features of the early atlases, which spanned little more than a decade between the late 1860s and early 1880s, were the lithographic depictions of the subscribers' homes, farms, and businesses. While often formulaic and sometimes displaying a primitive sense of proportion, these early real estate illustrations provide a fascinating perspective on the lives and aspirations of people in the rural Midwest. In many cases the structures they depict are no longer standing, but the illustrations show at least a depiction of the buildings around which our ancestors made their lives. More exciting is the possibility that the structures still stand, inviting us to return to the towns and back roads to compare the image of the sketch with what stands before us today.

DAVID THACKERY
Curator of Local and Family History,
The Newberry Library
Columnist, *Ancestry* magazine

Maps, atlases, and gazetteers are essential tools for family historians. Maps may be either topographical (emphasizing land forms) or historical (emphasizing historical events) in nature, though either type can show cultural features, such as the town and creek names that are so important for research. Public libraries and especially college and university libraries usually have good contemporary maps. Historical maps are sometimes more difficult to find. Genealogical and historical societies in the area you are researching are likely repositories for old maps. The Internet is also a good place to locate obscure  maps. (Ancestry.com adds one new map every day to its growing databases.)

FLESHING OUT THE STORY

It has never been enough for me to gather dates and places of my ancestors. I want to know what they were like, what their problems may have been, how they lived their lives. What can be learned about an ancestor's daily life patterns? How were they affected by transportation, occupations, dress, medical treatment, architecture, entertainment, education, religious practices, and ethnic traditions?

BEVERLY DELONG WHITAKER
In *Beyond Pedigrees:*
Organizing and Enhancing Your Work

At some point, usually sooner rather than later, every family historian arrives at a juncture where nothing more than names and dates can be found for ancestors. The further we go back in time, the harder it is to find information about individuals. Some of us go back just one generation and have difficulty finding any biographical information that will give us a glimpse of the real person. Many ghosts of the past remain just that because there are no surviving photographs, diaries, obituaries, biographical sketches in local histories, or surviving family members who can tell us what our ancestors were really like. Is it possible to know what these mysterious people were like? As Barbara MacPherson observed in "The Soul Beyond the Statistics: Discovering the Person Your Ancestor Was," *Ancestry* 13 (5): 5 (September/October 1995), "Social history is a new, exciting facet of historical research. Through it you should be able to find sources that focus on your particular area of interest. Social statistics can be very revealing when you compare your family with prevailing norms."

Once you have reached this point, the first step is to learn as much as you can about the place where your ancestors lived. Learn as much of the area's or country's history as possible. Beyond conventional history books, there are detailed sources on social history and statistics. Local histories of the areas in which your family lived make the most fascinating reading; it's almost like setting a stage and dropping the ancestor into place. The customs and surroundings take on new meaning, and so does the life of the individual. Through these sources you may learn about the locale, the kind of people who lived there, and more. Once you have the historical background in your mind, you will better understand the kinds of records that may have been created in the times and places where your people were present. Creating a historical time line with a parallel time line for an individual is an excellent way to put things into perspective.

Sample Timeline for James MILLER

Historical Background

Year	Event	Location	Sources to Check
1830	Father arrived in US	Port of New York	Passenger List
1832	Parents Married	Brooklyn, NY	Marriage record
1834	Birth	Brooklyn, NY	Baptism record
1837	Family moved twice	Financial panic—nationwide	Bankruptcy files?
1840	Father bought land	Kings County, NY	Land records
1850	Census, age 13	Kings County, NY	1850 census
1860	Census, age 22	Kings County, NY	1860 census
1861	Enlisted in army Civil War began		
1863	Mustered out of army		Military records
1870	wife and children listed, no James	Kings County, NY	1870 census

The Internet

The Internet is providing still more fascinating opportunities to add the historical background for your family story. If you want to see a photograph or a drawing of the town your family called home a hundred years ago, you may be able to visit a genealogical, historical, or other locally sponsored site and download a photograph that makes you feel like you are stepping right into your ancestor's life. Some of the sites also include historical chronologies that are good for quick reference. See chapter 10, "Family History, Computers, and the Internet."

Chapter Ten

$\mathscr{F}$AMILY $\mathscr{H}$ISTORY, $\mathscr{C}$OMPUTERS, AND THE $\mathscr{I}$NTERNET

COMPUTER PROGRAMS

Computers have become valuable tools for genealogists to store and disseminate the large amount of information they collect during the course of their research. There are now many genealogical programs on the market to help organize this data and make printing records a breeze. Once your family information has been entered, these programs will format it in various ways to print ancestor and descendant trees, family group sheets, kinship reports, ahnentafels, calendars, and more. Many allow you to include biographical sketches, photos, recipes, medical histories, video or audio clips, and more. Some programs will also format all of your information into scrapbooks that can be published or preserved for future generations in your family.

JULIANA S. SMITH
*The Ancestry Family Historian's
Address Book*

Genealogical software programs differ in various ways. There are articles and books to help you choose the program that is right for you. *Turbo Genealogy: An Introduction to Family History Research in the Information Age* by John and Carolyn Cosgriff is one such guide. *Genealogical Computing* quarterly is another excellent resource for the latest information on computer genealogy. There are also online newsletters, such as Dick Eastman's Online Genealogy Newsletter, that feature reviews of the newest versions of these software programs. These newsletters and where to find them will be discussed later in this chapter.

Most of these programs are GEDCOM-based. GEDCOM stands for Genealogical Data Communications. It is a computer standard for formatting genealogical data that enables users to transfer information among different software programs. An article by Lance Jacob titled "Everything You Wanted to Know about GEDCOM" is available at Ancestry.com (http://www.ancestry.com) to all visitors free of charge.

Because of the incredible rate at which these genealogical programs appear and are upgraded, any recommendations made here would be inappropriate. The best way to find out about these programs is to read the software and Internet reviews that are published regularly in genealogical publications. You can also visit the Web pages sponsored by the various software and Internet publishers. Then look at your own needs and decide for yourself.

THE INTERNET

The Internet isn't replacing the days spent rooting through the files in a dusty corner of a small-town courthouse, or wading through high grass to run cold fingers over a faded tombstone, or squinting at microfiche amidst the hum of a big library. But it will add a new dimension to your journey, and soon the flicker of a computer screen will become as familiar to you as your notebooks, file folders, and index cards.

LAURIE AND STEVE BONNER
In *Searching for Cyber-Roots*

Computers allow us to get to places we couldn't reach before. They let us store and retrieve information quickly and efficiently. But that's only the beginning. This new technology allows libraries, archives, genealogical and historical societies, genealogical publishers, government agencies, and museums, as well as individuals, to share their wealth of information with us.

The Internet is opening up a whole new world of research, and genealogists and historians, like researchers in every other field, are reaping this technological harvest. Federal, state, and county agencies, genealogical societies, historical societies, and individuals have Web sites where you can discover the scope of a collection, how to access more information, complete mailing addresses, telephone numbers, and sometimes downloadable forms and databases.

Going beyond the offerings of government and historical agencies, the Internet offers a wealth of tools and useful information: it is a window on the whole world. Genealogical societies and publishers have posted a vast array of guides and databases on their home pages. With the click of a button, you can see into the card catalog of a distant library, exchange research notes with a newly found cousin, download files from some sleepy town halfway across the world, or see photographs taken in the very time and place where your ancestors lived.

Where you begin your Internet investigation depends a great deal on your level of experience in conducting research and your experience with the Internet. Your goals will probably make your decision pretty easy. Is the information you seek at this time likely to be found in a federal, state, or local agency? Perhaps a genealogical society can guide you to specific resources. Maybe you're searching for help on just one surname. In any case, a well-planned strategy can save both the experienced and novice researcher valuable time. With literally millions of people and sources on the Internet and more being added daily, a visit to the Internet can be like a visit to the jungle. It's easy to get lost.

THE WORLD WIDE WEB

Search Engines

> *Without some guidance, using the World Wide Web to find information is an exercise in educated guessing. In a way, the same problems often exist in print. A large and valuable manuscript collection is a daunting obstacle if no one has taken the time to index its contents. Indexes and catalogs help us to find information quickly because they lend additional organization to the data they describe. Fortunately, similar finding aids exist on the Internet. These indexes are called search engines. Each search engine is different in terms of organization and coverage; each indexes Web sites in a slightly different manner; and each interprets your request differently. Dozens of search engines now exist, yet only a handful stand out as fast, comprehensive, powerful tools. It is important to find a search engine you are comfortable with. Experiment with several to find the one that you feel works best for you.*

> JAKE GEHRING
> In *Ancestry* magazine

The following are some well-known search engines:

AltaVista
http://www.altavista.digital.com/
(Indexes Usenet news groups as well as the World Wide Web and is updated often)

Excite
http://www.excite.com/
(Big on features, speed, and accuracy; very comprehensive)

HotBot
http://www.hotbot.com/
(Fully automated; fast growing; good search features)

Lycos
http://www.lycos.com/
(Complete searching; includes additional features such as PeopleFind and CityGuide)

MetaCrawler
http://www.metacrawler.com/
(Searches Lycos, Excite, Yahoo!, HotBot and other search engines simultaneously)

Yahoo!
http://www.yahoo.com/
(Hierarchically organized; extremely popular)

All search engines are not equal. In doing a search, it is important to note that the criteria entered may bring up different results in different search engines. Many search engines are equipped with "smart" functions which can look for variations of a word, determine that Robert equals Bob, or even establish relationships between words or phrases (for example, elderly people equals senior citizens). Despite this, a search for naturalizations may produce different results than a search for naturalization records. So don't give up if your first search doesn't result in the information that you need. Try some variations or experiment with a different search engine.

Directories
Whether you're looking for a long-lost cousin or the address of the library in your ancestor's hometown, there are quite a few online directories to assist in your search, both locally and internationally. Here are some of my favorites.

Domestic
BigBook
http://bigbook.com/

Bigfoot
http://www.bigfoot.com/

BigYellow
http://www1.bigyellow.com/

Four11
http://www.four11.com/

Switchboard
http://www.switchboard.com

WhoWhere
http://www.whowhere.com/

555-1212
http://www.555-1212.com/

International
Online phonebooks of the world, by Bob Coret
http://www.coret.demon.nl/phone/

Telephone Directories on the Web
http://www.contractjobs.com/tel/

HISTORICAL BACKGROUND

> *With this mouse on our computers, we can click in a name—*
> *and instantly see our ancestors' names appear on our screens*
> *in our genealogy programs. With a mouse we can drag and*
> *drop a photo of our ancestors into a genealogy chart or a fam-*
> *ily history. With a mouse we can trip from Web page to Web*
> *page and travel from Fort Wayne to Frankfort, and Dallas to*
> *Duesseldorf, following our ancestors around the World.*

TONY BURROUGHS
President, Black Roots

U.S. HISTORY

The Library of Congress (http://lcweb.loc.gov/) is a valuable
tool for genealogists. Its catalogs are extraordinary resources for
finding publications. There is a collection of Civil War photographs (part of the American Memory Collection) containing
1,118 photographs. The subjects can be searched or browsed
and reproductions can be ordered from the site. There are also
various historical exhibitions available online. This site is truly a
national treasure and well worth a visit.

For information on ancestors who lived in the United
States, the Library of Congress's American Memory Project is
an outstanding resource. The exhibitions range from textual references to audio files to actual video footage. Among the videos
is actual footage of immigrants arriving at Ellis Island.

LOWER EAST SIDE TENEMENT MUSEUM

Imagine that a family has made it through the gates of Ellis Island, its members have passed their inspections, and now they're looking for a place to stay in New York. They may have found refuge on the Lower East Side with many other immigrants. The Lower East Side Tenement Museum (http://www.wnet.org/archive/tenement/) has a virtual tour of a few tenement apartments and some insight into the lives of the residents. You can visit the museum, learn the history of the place, and view a movie, all without leaving your home.

CIVIL WAR

Did one or more of your ancestors serve in the Civil War? There is a plethora of information on the Web about every aspect of the war. Some good starting points are:

Civil War Soldiers and Sailors System
http://www.itd.nps.gov/cwss/

The U.S. Civil War Center
http://www.cwc.lsu.edu/

TRAILS

Among Web sites that follow pioneers on their westward journey is the Oregon California Trails Association (OCTA) (http://cacite.rocky.edu/octa3/octahome.htm). OCTA is actively involved in promoting education about the westward emigrant experience and the trails themselves. These efforts involve several publications that are available through the Web site.

ORPHAN TRAINS

Many events in history that helped shape our ancestors' lives may provide valuable clues about migration patterns. The orphan trains of the 1850s are a good example.

The direction of institutional care of orphans and neglected children changed course in the mid-nineteenth century. A trial placement of abandoned city children on farms in rural New York and nearby Connecticut proved successful, encouraging placement on a larger scale. In 1854, forty-seven boys and girls between the ages of seven and fifteen boarded a train in New York City; they were destined for a rural community in southwestern Michigan. This was the beginning of an exodus that transferred well over 100,000 homeless children from cities such as Boston, New York, and Cincinnati to entirely different lifestyles in small towns and farms in states in the Midwest, the South, and the West.

JOHNI CERNY
"Research in Business, Employment,
and Institutional Records"
In *The Source: A Guidebook of American Genealogy*

More information on the orphan trains, as well as newspaper accounts, partial lists of the children and the institutions that they came from, and more, can be found at:

Orphan Trains of Kansas
   http://kuhttp.cc.ukans.edu/carrie/kancoll/articles/
      orphans/index.html

ETHNIC/FOREIGN HISTORY

African American
Opened in 1976, the Afro-American Historical and Cultural Museum is the first major museum devoted specifically to African American history and tradition. Visit the Web site at http://www.fieldtrip.com/pa/55740380.htm.

German
If you're studying German emigration from Europe, you may wish to visit Michael Palmer's "German and American Sources for German Emigration to America" site at http://www. Genealogy.com/gene/.

Hungarian
For Hungarian history, you can turn to Hunyadi Matyas Kozosseg, Hungarian History, from the Corvinus Library. This virtual library contains a wealth of history on the Austro-Hungarian regions at http://www.net.hu/corvinus/.

Irish
For an understanding of what Irish immigrants experienced, there are several fascinating Web sites, including:

A Commemoration of the Great Famine (Ireland 1845)
http://www.pilot.infi.net/~cksmith/famine/PotatCom.html

Interpreting the Irish Famine: 1846–1850
http://avery.med.virginia.edu/~eas5e/Irish/Famine.html

William Bennett's Narrative of a Recent Journey of Six
    Weeks in Ireland (1847)
http://avery.med.virginia.edu/~eas5e/Irish/bennett.html

Robert Whyte's The Journey of an Irish Coffin Ship (1847)
http://avery.med.virginia.edu/~eas5e/Irish/RWhyte.html

Polish
If you have Polish ancestry, you'll probably want to visit the Polish Genealogical Society of America's Web site. It has a history section that includes information on various aspects of Polish history at http://www.pgsa.org.

OTHER POSSIBILITIES
Maybe your ancestors don't fit one of these categories, but no matter what your family's background, there's a good chance that you'll be able to gain some insight into their lives by traveling back in time through an Internet site. Almost every ethnic group has some representation on the Internet. The sites mentioned here were easily found by using search engines. If you don't get immediate results, experiment with different search engines or different search terminology.

MAPS

Maps are valuable tools for genealogists. There are many Web sites with interactive atlases from today and yesterday, and for the United States and abroad. Many countries' boundaries have changed—in some cases more than once—and it is important to be able to know exactly where ancestors were living in a given time in order to find their records. In the United States, state and county borders have changed, and town names have changed (some towns have ceased to exist altogether). These are but a few of the problems that can be solved by the use of maps.

One way to check for local maps online is to use a search engine. For instance, a search on Metacrawler for "New York historical map" turned up a site from the State University of New York (SUNY)/Stony Brook's Map Collection at http://www.coret.demon.nl/phone/. This page contains links to twenty historical maps beginning with one from 1556 Giacomo di Gastaldi, of New France, and ending with an 1895 Rand McNally map of New York.

Below are some other map sites that you may find useful in your research.

Ancestry.com
http://www.ancestry.com (Ancestry.com adds one map to
    its database every day.)

1895 U.S. Atlas by Pam Rietsch
http://www.ismi.net/lcmigw/1895.htm

Cartographic links on Internet from the Department of
    Cartography, Eötvös University, Budapest
http://lazarus.elte.hu/gb/linkek.htm

Color Landform Atlas of the United States
http://fermi.jhuapl.edu/states/states.html

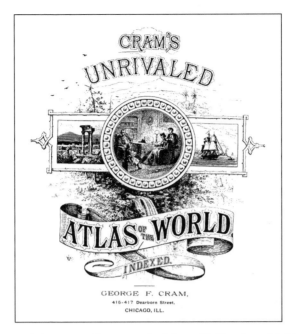

Library of Congress Panoramic Maps Collection 1847–1925
http://lcweb2.loc.gov/ammem/pmhtml/panhome.html

List of Historical Map Web Sites from the Perry-Castañeda
    Library Map Collection, The University of Texas at
    Austin
http://www.lib.utexas.edu/Libs/PCL/Mapcollection/
    mapsites/histsites.html

Mapblast!
http://www.mapblast.com/

Mapquest
http://www.mapquest.com/

U.S. Geological Survey, Geographic Names Information
    System
http://mapping.usgs.gov/www/gnis/gnisform.html

ONLINE GENEALOGY CLASSES

There are now a number of free genealogy classes available on the Internet. Ancestry.com (http://www.ancestry.com) has an Academy where lessons are offered on a variety of topics, such as Genealogy for Beginners, Using LDS Family History Centers, Let's Get Organized, and U.S. Genealogy State Lessons. There are also sample articles from *Genealogical Computing*.

Another good source is the International Internet Genealogical Society's University (http://www.iigs.org/university/). It has classes for general instruction and some classes arranged by geographic region.

THE USGENWEB PROJECT

This outstanding resource at http://www.usgenweb.com is the work of volunteers who are creating sites for every state and county in the United States. These pages contain a wealth of valuable information for the genealogist. On the main page you'll find links to state pages that feature valuable information on many state resources, as well as links to various county pages. The county pages vary in content and are as individual as the volunteers who create them. Many contain databases, directories, and indexes of various types, including cemetery transcriptions, Civil War rosters, census records, and more. They also contain links and addresses for other local resources, as well as a query page and/or surname directory where you can submit your own queries or surnames. The main page also contains valuable information—for example, links to other resources, Answers to Common Problems/Questions, Researching Helps (including Helpful Hints for Beginning Researchers), and Care of Old Documents. Other features include information on various USGenWeb special projects, such as the Archives Project, which is striving to place public domain records online so that they will be freely accessible to all researchers; the Census Project, which is putting census data online; the Military

Records Project, which endeavors to collect military records and transcribe them for online access; and the Tombstone Project, which is compiling cemetery data online. These pages are excellent resources for researchers of every level.

MAILING LISTS AND NEWSGROUPS

Mailing lists and newsgroups are forums in which users can exchange information relating to the subjects for which they are formed. First, let's distinguish the two. Newsgroups are accessed through a newsreader program on your Web browser. You subscribe to the newsgroup of your choice and read the various postings through your newsreader at your leisure. If you're on a mailing list, individual pieces of mail come right to your in box.

Many mailing lists and newsgroups are available for genealogists. They can be broken down by geographic region, ethnic group, surnames, or any number of research levels and types. There are software and commercial lists, immigrant lists, "newbie" (beginner) lists, and many more. There are several sites that offer lists of these mailing lists. Here are a few:

Genealogy Resources on the Internet by John Fuller and Christine Gaunt (mailing lists)
http://users.aol.com/johnf14246/gen_mail.html

Genealogy Resources on the Internet by John Fuller and Christine Gaunt (Usenet newsgroups)
http://users.aol.com/johnf14246/gen_use.html

Rootsweb Mailing Lists
http://www.rootsweb.com/~maillist/

These groups are wonderful sources for making contact with other researchers who have similar research interests; for learning of new resources; and maybe even for finding a long-

lost cousin! Remember, though: a lot of misinformation can be passed around in these forums. Many rumors have spread to epidemic proportions, only to be proved completely untrue.

EASTMAN'S ONLINE GENEALOGY NEWSLETTER

Eastman's Online Genealogy Newsletter, offered free of charge at Ancestry.com, is a weekly collection of news and notes about "what is happening now in the world of genealogy" by popular online celebrity Dick Eastman.

> *The weekly newsletters include information about new genealogy software, new genealogy CD-ROM disks, genealogy conventions and meetings around the world, and other items of interest to genealogists. You will also read what the "rumor mill" is saying this week. The newsletter will keep you up-to-date on many issues of importance and interest to genealogists.*
>
> DICK EASTMAN, AUTHOR
> Forum manager of the
> four genealogy forums on CompuServe
> Editor of *Genealogical Computing*

No other publication can give you reviews of new genealogy software the same week they're released! (Sometimes the newsletter even has an in-depth review before a program is released.)

While most of the news items in Eastman's Online Genealogy Newsletter are related to the use of computers in genealogy research, some are about other topics that are closely related.

INDEXES AND DATABASES

Genealogical and historical organizations, genealogical companies, individuals, and, as mentioned before, the USGenWeb Project have all been building databases, any of which may contain the unique piece of information you need to complete the biography of an individual or the history of a family. It's very important to remember that information on the Internet is not monitored and thus may not always be entirely accurate or complete. Verify any information you obtain from a database by comparing it with actual records.

One source for databases is Ancestry.com (http://www. ancestry.com), where a new database is added every day. Each database is free for ten days, after which it is moved to the subscriber area. Quarterly and annual subscriptions are available.

Also available in the subscriber area is *PERSI* (the *Periodical Source Index*), produced by the Allen County Public Library in Indiana. *PERSI* is a comprehensive subject index to genealogy and local history periodicals written in English and French-Canadian since 1800. The collection also includes literature dating from the 1700s (although the collection is less complete for pre-1800 articles). *PERSI* does not index every name in every article, nor does it include the full text of actual articles; however, it does indicate the publisher of each periodical. If the publisher no longer exists, you can check with your local library or historical society for availability of the periodical. You can also contact the Allen County Public Library, which owns a copy of each periodical indexed in *PERSI*, for photocopies of the article.

Among the free databases you can find at Ancestry.com is the *Social Security Death Index (SSDI)*. It contains more than 50 million records created from Social Security Administration payment records. A successful search will reward the user with last name, first name, Social Security number, state issued, birth date, death date, last residence, and lump sum payment.

The World Family Tree is also available at the site, free of charge. You can also submit your genealogy in GEDCOM format so that others may view it and possibly connect with you.

A database of links is available on the Ancestry.com site at "Juliana's Links." You can search for links to other sites using specific criteria, such as geographic location, record type, ethnic or religious group, or miscellaneous (which includes genealogical or historical societies, libraries, government agencies, immigration sites, software/hardware/shareware, and many other categories).

GOVERNMENT AGENCIES

Government Web pages are excellent sources for information on the federal, state, and local levels. The National Archives and Records Administration (NARA) (http://www.nara.gov/) has an elaborate system of pages with much information for the genealogist. Although it will be years before a significant portion of the genealogical records available from the NARA are online, there are numerous research guides that can help researchers prepare for a trip to one of the many facilities. Below are some of the helpful pages from the NARA.

The Genealogy Page
http://www.nara.gov/genealogy/genindex.html
(This page provides links to information on Census Records; Military Service Records; Immigrant and Passenger Arrivals; Genealogical and Biographical Research; Federal Court Records;

American Indians; Black Studies; Microfilm Resources for
Research: A Comprehensive Catalog; links to Regional Records
Services Facilities; and links to several other helpful sites.)

NARA Archival Information Locator (NAIL)
http://www.nara.gov/nara/nail.html
(NAIL is the working prototype for a future online catalog of
holdings in Washington, D.C., the National Archives' regional
archives, and the Presidential libraries. Until a full catalog is
developed, NAIL will continue to serve as the agency's online
information system. It currently contains descriptions of fifty-
two thousand Cherokee, Creek, and Seminole applications for
enrollment to the Five Civilized Tribes (Dawes Commission)
between 1898 and 1914 and descriptions of fifty thousand Fort
Smith, Arkansas, criminal case files.)

Information Sources in the National Archives Library
http://www.nara.gov/nara/naralibrary/refmenu.html
(Information on the collections available at the National
Archives Library)

Keep an open mind; sometimes the original source may not
be the best source of information. A good example is
the Immigration and Naturalization Service (INS)
(http://www.ins.usdoj.gov/). Although its home page has some
information and forms for requesting records, I found a site for
Jewish Genealogy (http://www.jewishgen.org/faqinfo.html)
that explained the process of requesting forms from the INS
and offered alternatives that could yield faster results.

Every state has a Web page at http://www.state.__.us/. (Insert
the appropriate two-letter state abbreviation in the blank.) This
page usually provides links to many state agencies, including
those responsible for vital records (which sometimes contain
downloadable forms for requesting various vital records) and the
state library (often provides a directory of libraries in the state,
genealogical research guides, online catalogs, state historical soci-

eties, and more). The Web pages of many state archives can also provide valuable information regarding the collections they hold, and many are now offering online databases as well. The Illinois State Archives' Web page, for example, now features the Database of Illinois Civil War Veterans, which contains the names of approximately 250,000 men (http://www.sos.state.il.us/depts/archives/datcivil.html), and the Database of Illinois Spanish-American War Veterans, which contains the names of approximately 11,000 men (http://www.sos.state.il.us/depts/archives/spanam.html). Many other state archives have online catalogs, genealogy pages with valuable research guides, research services, and much more. The West Virginia State Archives maintains a page with links to other state archives at http://www.wvlc.wvnet.edu/history/linkarch.html.

There is much information to be found at the county level as well. The Albany County Hall of Records in New York, for example (http://www.albanycounty.com/achor/index.htm), now has some county naturalization indexes for 1821 to 1850 online, and its creators hope to add an Index to Corning Papers and an Abstract of Wills, 1787 to 1800, soon.

Foreign government Web sites can also be a great source of information. The National Archives of Ireland (http://www.kst.dit.ie/nat-arch/index.html) has transportation records of convicts sent from Ireland to Australia between 1788 and 1868 online, a family history and genealogy page, information on the Great Famine, a business records survey, and archives of the Ordnance Survey of Ireland containing searchable lists of records and documents produced in the nineteenth century, including an index of parish names. There is also a list of links to other archives around the world. The National Archives of Canada (http://www.archives.ca/www/Genealogy.html) has a database index of the Canadian Expeditionary Force during the First World War, an index to the 1871 Census of Ontario, and a helpful guide to genealogical sources in Canada.

LIBRARIES AND ONLINE CATALOGS

How many times have you gone to a library and spent hours poring over a computerized catalog or card index looking for holdings that pertain to your research? Wouldn't it be easier to sit at home and browse the catalog via your home computer? Many libraries' Web sites offer access to these valuable catalogs, and even if the entire catalog is not available, many times an overview of the collection is available. Often, you can contact the library by e-mail ahead of time to find out if the resources in question are available. If a library is undergoing renovations and will be closed or have unusual hours, this information should be found at the Web site, as will its regular hours of operation and restrictions. Before a research trip, it is always helpful to check the Web page.

There is often a directory of libraries with links to Web pages at the state library page. Web addresses for many libraries are also available at Juliana's Links at http://www.ancestry.com.

___ration of Genealogical Societies
http://www.fgs.org/~fgs/
(Links and information on the various members from all across the United States, current events, news on records preservation issues.)

Immigrant Genealogical Society
http://feefhs.org/igs/frg-igs.html
(First immigrants list, databases, research services.)

National Genealogical Society
http://www.ngsgenealogy.org/
(Genealogical forms and research aids, genealogists' guide to the Internet, tips for beginners, Journal of Online Genealogy, links.)

U.S. Internet Genealogical Society
http://www.usigs.org/
(Resources listed nationally and by state.)

ETHNIC/INTERNATIONAL GENEALOGICAL RESOURCES

Association of European Migration Institutions
http://users.cybercity.dk/~ccc13652/
("Institutions and organizations in Europe, whose field of interest concern migration, research, and exhibitions portraying emigration, and who seek to promote understanding of common goals..."; addresses and links to members, which include museums, archives, institutes, etc., across Europe.)

Australian Archives' Genealogical Records
http://www.aa.gov.au/AA_WWW/AA_Holdings/AA_Genie/Genie.html
(Information on records available, including naturalization, passenger lists, migrant selection documents; database to allow

users access to detailed information about the records held and the agencies that created them.)

Australian Migration and Naturalizations—LDS Microform Copies
   http://www.zeta.org.au/~feraltek/lists/ldsmigr.htm
   (Migration and Naturalization records available through LDS libraries.)

AVOTAYNU
   http://www.avotaynu.com/
   (Information on publications, maps, links.)

Cunard Archives: Information on Passengers and Emigrants
   http://www.liv.ac.uk/~archives/cunard/chome.htm
   (Archives of the Cunard Steamship Company, established in 1840, which carried many immigrants to America.)

Federation of Eastern European Family History Societies (FEEFHS)
   http://feefhs.org/
   (Excellent resource page with many valuable links, Internet journal, maps, and more.)

GENUKI—Genealogy in the U.K. and Ireland
   http://midas.ac.uk/genuki/
   (Tips on getting started; good links to resources in the U.K. and Ireland, including information on immigration/emigration resources and much more.)

German and American Sources for German Emigration to America
   by Michael P. Palmer
   http://www.genealogy.com/gene/www/emig/emigrati.htm
   (List of German emigrant resources.)

Irish Emigrants
http://genealogy.org/~ajmorris/ireland/ireemg1.htm
(List of Irish emigrants.)

Jewish Genealogy
http://www.jewishgen.org/
(Answers some basic questions about Jewish genealogy;
databases; Jewish Cemetery Project online; Jewish Family
Finder; includes information on naturalizations.)

Norway/Son og Fjordane: The Emigration Archives
http://fjordinfo.vestdata.no/offentleg/sffarkiv/sffut1.htm
(Contains an online migration database, 1839 to 1924, and
other information on emigrants from Norway.)

ODESSA...A German-Russian Genealogical Library
http://pixel.cs.vt.edu/library/odessa.html
(Library and repository with much information including
immigration, naturalization, and ship records; also some declarations of intentions listed online.)

ODIN-Ministry of Foreign Affairs
How To Trace Your Ancestors in Norway
http://odin.dep.no/ud/publ/96/ancestors/
(Contains general information on preparation and procedures, lists various sources of information.)

Palatines to America
http://genealogy.org/~palam/
(This organization has an "On-line Immigrant Ancestor
Register," a quarterly journal, and a newsletter, as well as
regional publications; also links to other sites.)

Swenson Swedish Immigration Research Center
http://www2.augustana.edu/admin/swenson/

(Information about collections and publications; links to other sites including some Scandinavian immigration.)

LINKS TO PASSENGER LISTS/IMMIGRANT INFORMATION

Emigration/Ship Lists and Resources
http://www.geocities.com/Heartland/5978/Emigration.html
(Links to various passenger lists and immigrant/emigrant information.)

GENEALOGY RESOURCES ON THE INTERNET

Passenger Lists; Ships; Ship Museums
http://www-personal.umich.edu/~cgaunt/pass.html
(Links to information about researching passenger lists, information in archives, information about ships, individual ships, and disasters.)

Library of Michigan—Bibliography of Immigrant/Passenger Lists
http://www.libofmich.lib.mi.us/genealogy/immigration.html
(Lists various printed sources.)

The Olive Tree Genealogy—Index to Passenger Lists
http://www.rootsweb.com/~ote/indexshp.htm
(Index to various ship passenger lists; information and links to other books and resources.)

OTHER GENERAL GENEALOGICAL SITES

American Genealogical Lending Library (AGLL)
http://www.agll.com/
(Seven steps to a family tree; newsletter.)

Ancestry.com
http://www.ancestry.com/
(Many searchable databases, several with immigration information; links to other sources; online genealogy newsletters; National Archives Research Guide; *PERSI*—Online Genealogical Periodical Search; World Tree; Genealogy Academy with genealogy classes; Social Security Death Index Online; links to professional researchers; information on publications and sales online; new database added daily; and more.)

Cyndi's List of Genealogical Sites on the Internet
http://www.oz.net/~cyndihow/sites.htm
(Categorized links to more than twenty thousand genealogy-related sites.)

Everton's Genealogical Helper
http://www.everton.com/
(Online searches, databases, newsletter online, links.)

Family Tree Maker
http://www.familytreemaker.com/
(Beginners class online, Family Finder indexes and searches, orders for record searches.)

Frontier Press
http://www.doit.com/frontier/
(Information on publications and book sales online.)

Genealogy Home Page
http://genhomepage.com/
(Categorized links to resources.)

Rand Genealogy Club
http://www.rand.org/personal/Genea
(Categorized links including some immigration resources.)

These are exciting times that we live in. With technology advancing exponentially—every couple of moments, it seems—and with more and more individuals coming into the field of genealogy, we have a convergence of some really wonderful things: a lot of talent, a lot of opportunities, and a lot of possibilities, and some technology to help us manage those opportunities.

CURT WITCHER, MANAGER,
Historical Genealogy Department
Allen County Public Library
Fort Wayne, Indiana

STANDARDS FOR USE OF TECHNOLOGY IN GENEALOGICAL RESEARCH,

Recommended by the National Genealogical Society

Mindful that computers are tools, genealogists take full responsibility for their work, and therefore they:

- learn the capabilities and limits of their equipment and software, and use them only when they are the most appropriate tools for a purpose;
- refuse to let computer software automatically embellish their work;
- treat compiled information from online sources or digital databases like that from other published sources, useful primarily as a guide to locating original records, but not as evidence for a conclusion or assertion;
- accept digital images or enhancements of an original record as a satisfactory substitute for the original only when there is reasonable assurance that the image accurately reproduces the unaltered original;
- cite sources for data obtained online or from digital media with the same care that is appropriate for sources on paper and other traditional media, and enter data into a digital database only when its source can remain associated with it;

- always cite the sources for information or data posted online or sent to others, naming the author of a digital file as its immediate source, while crediting original sources cited within the file;
- preserve the integrity of their own databases by evaluating the reliability of downloaded data before incorporating it into their own files;
- provide, whenever they alter data received in digital form, a description of the change that will accompany the altered data whenever it is shared with others;
- actively oppose the proliferation of error, rumor, and fraud by personally verifying or correcting information, or noting it as unverified, before passing it on to others;
- treat people online as courteously and civilly as they would treat them face-to-face, not separated by networks and anonymity;
- and accept that technology has not changed the principles of genealogical research, only some of the procedures.

SELECTED READING

One of the best sources for staying current with developments is *Genealogical Computing (GC)* quarterly. *GC* has a staple of well-known contributing authors, all recognized for their expertise in both genealogy and computer technology. Intended for the beginner as well as the advanced family historian, each issue presents new information and product reviews. *Genealogical Computing* is available four times a year from Ancestry, P.O. Box 476, Salt Lake City, UT 84110. Call 1-800-Ancestry or order from www.ancestry.com.

Bonner, Laurie, and Steve Bonner. *Searching for Cyber-Roots: A Step-by-Step Guide to Genealogy on the World Wide Web.* Salt Lake City: Ancestry, 1997. (Provides insights into the fascinating history of the Web and a guide to the wonderful genealogical resources that are available online.)

Cosgriff, John, and Carolyn Cosgriff. *Turbo Genealogy: An Introduction to Family History Research in the Information Age.* Salt Lake City: Ancestry, 1997. (Chapter 9, "Basic Computer Hardware," is an especially useful chapter for computer beginners.)

Smith, Juliana Szucs. *The Ancestry Family Historian's Address Book: A Comprehensive List of Local, State, and Federal Agencies and Institutions and Ethnic and Genealogical Organizations.* Salt Lake City: Ancestry, 1998. (Has the most extensive list of genealogical addresses, URLs, and e-mail addresses in print.)

Chapter Eleven

&DUCATIONAL AND
&ROFESSIONAL &PPORTUNITIES

*Genealogy—good genealogy—requires constant growth,
which comes in two ways: education and practice. Neither
alone is sufficient. Used together, they are synergistic. Learn
about a skill or resource, then get out there and apply it.
That's how we become better genealogists.*

PATRICIA LAW HATCHER, CG
Producing a Quality Family History

There are exciting educational and professional opportunities in genealogy and family history. The possibilities for learning more and finding a career in this ever-expanding field are great for beginning and seasoned family historians. Depending on where you live, there may be occasional genealogical lectures or regular classes—usually sponsored by public libraries, community colleges, or genealogical societies. Professional organizations and universities offer specialized courses for those who wish to turn genealogical research into a career. More and more classes are being offered on the Internet, including those offered at Ancestry.com.

As Pat Hatcher noted in "Educational Opportunities in Genealogy," *Ancestry* 14 (3) (May-June 1996), "A popular and inexpensive form of genealogical learning is available through the continuing education programs of local colleges or junior colleges." As she also points out, not only do continuing education classes get researchers off on the right foot, but friendships with other class members and instructors with similar interests can often be even more valuable than the information imparted in the study.

According to Sharon DeBartolo Carmack in *The Genealogy Sourcebook*, "National conferences are the perfect places not only to get an education, but also to network and talk with people." National and larger state and local conferences offer two or three days of concurrent sessions that attract thousands of researchers of virtually every level of experience. Most of the lectures are recorded and may be purchased from audiotape recording companies and from some genealogical vendors.

GENEALOGICAL SOCIETIES: THEIR PUBLICATIONS AND EDUCATIONAL OPPORTUNITIES

Genealogical societies hold regular meetings (usually monthly), workshops, and conferences at which specialists speak on topics such as how to best locate and use local records efficiently and using special kinds of records (such as court records, military records, newspapers, land records, and coroners' records) most efficiently. Frequently, genealogical societies collaborate with local archives, historical societies, grade schools, high schools, colleges and universities, and libraries to sponsor workshops and classes.

Most societies publish monthly newsletters to keep members current on local projects, events, and issues that favorably or negatively affect national and local genealogical research. In addition to newsletters, almost all genealogical societies publish quarterly journals in which essays on research methodology are featured. Local records, historical events, and historical figures

and families are usually the predominant themes of these publications. Quarterly publications often contain society-sponsored indexing projects, such as cemetery, census, or naturalization records, for the area served by the society. Book reviews that focus on publications having wide (national) appeal and publications that focus on the locality served are other good reasons for joining a genealogical society.

As noted in chapter 6, "Genealogical Societies," joining an organized group is important if for no other reason than to become "registered" as a family historian. If the number of people involved in family history is as great as polls and resulting statistics indicate, there is an enormous demand and marketplace for genealogy-related materials. Tangible figures, however, such as those based on genealogical society membership rolls, are what public institutions, private companies, and major corporations rely on when they decide the feasibility of backing products, projects, and programs that will benefit not only genealogical but historical interest.

GENEALOGICAL INSTITUTES

Some organizations sponsor week-long institutes—intensive, multi-track programs oriented toward a variety of interests and skill levels. The best-known institutes are the Institute of Genealogy and Historical Research (held every June in Birmingham, Alabama), the Genealogical Institute of Mid-America (July in Springfield, Illinois), the National Institute of Genealogical Research (July in Washington, D.C.), and the Institute of Genealogical Studies (July in the Dallas, Texas, area). In 1996, institutes were begun in Salt Lake City, Utah, and in Rosslyn, Virginia. Also in 1996, a summer camp was conducted in Philadelphia, and the Disney Institute added genealogy to its program selections for guests at Walt Disney World resorts in Orlando. Another popular option is a conference offered every August by Brigham Young University; it offers ten different tracks over four days.

HOME STUDY COURSES

For those who prefer not to travel, a home study course, American Genealogy: A Basic Course, is offered by the National Genealogical Society (NGS). The Basic Course, which is accredited by the Accrediting Commission of the Distance Education and Training Council, provides sixteen lessons covering information that can be found in records and how to find, document, and describe findings. Assigned instructors review your assignments and make comments. There is a payment structure for members and nonmembers.

Another well-respected independent study course is that offered by Brigham Young University in Provo, Utah. This course, which confers accreditation or certification, is excellent preparation for those who wish to attain those credentials. Those who successfully complete an eighteen-credit hour BYU home study course earn a distinct certificate.

The Internet is making home education a popular option. Michael Neill teaches a class through Carl Sandburg College in Galesburg, Illinois, titled "Genealogy on the Internet." It has offerings for beginning and intermediate students. Weekly lectures are posted, and assignments and instructor feedback are available at http://csc.tech-center.org/~mneill/csc.html. Addresses for these institutions can be found at the end of this chapter. Other Internet educational opportunities are described in chapter 10.

National genealogical conferences are held annually in different parts of the United States. For information regarding NGS conference schedules, write to the National Genealogical Society at the address given at the end of this chapter. For information regarding the annual conference held by the Federation of Genealogical Societies (FGS), write to the Federation of Genealogical Societies, P.O. Box 830220, Richardson, TX 75083-0220. The publications of these two organizations, the *NGS Newsletter* and the FGS *Forum*, provide in-depth information (including multi-page programs) about their respective conferences in appropriate issues. The *Forum* maintains an international calendar of major events with contact information.

PERIODICALS

In addition to the genealogical publications mentioned before, there are other worthwhile genealogical periodicals that offer educational and professional opportunities. *Ancestry*, a full-color, bimonthly magazine, offers regular columns by nationally respected genealogists, historical articles, a computer column, stories submitted by family historians from around the world, notices of new genealogical books, and case studies written by readers showing how they have resolved unusual genealogical research problems.

Genealogical Computing quarterly is unique in that it addresses the growing role of computers in genealogy. With world-renowned contributing authors, and edited by authority Dick Eastman, *GC* is published quarterly by Ancestry. Other popular commercial periodicals include Everton's *Genealogical Helper*, *Family Chronicle*, and *Heritage Quest*. Unfortunately, you won't find many genealogical periodicals in bookstores or on newsstands—even where almost every other interest, hobby, and profession is well represented. Addresses for the publications appear at the end of this chapter.

PROFESSIONAL GROUPS

In the United States, there are several groups that serve the interests of professional genealogists and their clients. The Association of Professional Genealogists (P.O. Box 40393, Denver, CO 80204-0393 or apg-admin@apgen.org <http://www.apgen.org/~apg/>) is a membership organization that does not administer tests, award credentials, or otherwise endorse individual researchers. (The association does offer arbitration in the event of a dispute between any association member and the genealogical public.) A publication that lists members' names, addresses, and areas of expertise is the *APG Directory of Professional Genealogists*. It is revised every two years and can be ordered from the APG office.

INSTITUTIONS THAT GRANT CREDENTIALS

> *The two major independent organizations that test genealo-gists are the Family History Library (FHL) in Salt Lake City, Utah, which grants accreditation, and the Board for Certification of Genealogists (BCG) in Washington, D.C., which grants certification. Other genealogy credentials are granted by colleges which provide a certificate of completion (Monterey Peninsula College and Hartnell College in California are two in this category), and universities which grant a degree in Family History (Brigham Young University is the largest). Each of these programs has different assessment procedures, different requirements, and different ways of defin-ing areas of specialization within the genealogical field.*
>
> KAREN CLIFFORD, AG
> President, Genealogy Research Associates
> In *Becoming an Accredited Genealogist*

Whether it is for the pure satisfaction of having achieved something, for the privilege of having some initials behind your name, or whether it is the need for more credibility to earn a living, many genealogists want to know more about the processes involved in the granting of credentials. In her book *Becoming an Accredited Genealogist: Plus 100 Tips to Ensure Your Success*, Karen Clifford observes that becoming an accredited, certified, or degreed genealogist can be a major step to a lucra-tive career in genealogy. Understanding very early in the research process what is involved in getting those credentials is a tremendous advantage.

The following ideas expand upon Clifford's list of benefits associated with credentials:

Free advertising: Being included with other credentialed researchers on lists and in directories that are mailed to thousands of interested individuals and libraries.

Advancement: Credentials sometimes make it easier to open career paths in independent genealogical research, writing, publishing, teaching, lecturing, heraldry consulting, investigating missing heirs, and detective and adoption research work. Specialists in tracing lineages, Native American, African American, and every kind of ethnic research are finding increasing opportunities in this field. Technology is opening doors to exciting opportunities for genealogical software developers, database developers, and computer genealogy instructors.

Confidence: Obtaining professional credentials is a great confidence booster—you know you have met the professional standards of the bestowing institution.

Certificates and cards: Certificates bestowed can be displayed, but perhaps more importantly, a card that identifies you as a professional will sometimes allow you to see records that are not otherwise open to the general public.

Credentials awarded:

AG:	Accredited Genealogist
CG:	Certified Genealogist
CGIC:	Certified Genealogical Instructor
CGL:	Certified Genealogical Lecturer
CGRS:	Certified Genealogical Record Specialist
CALS:	Certified American Lineage Specialist
CAILS:	Certified American Indian Lineage Specialist

SELECTED ADDRESSES

Ancestry Incorporated
P.O. Box 476
Salt Lake City, UT 84110

or
266 West Center Street
Orem, UT 84058
1-800-ANCESTRY or 1-801-426-3500
http://www.ancestry.com

Accredited Genealogists
Family History Library
35 North West Temple
Salt Lake City, UT 84150

Association of Professional Genealogists
P.O. Box 40393
Denver, CO 80204-0393
e-mail: apg-admin@apgen.org
http://www.apgen.org/~apg/

Board for Certification of Genealogists
P.O. Box 14291
Washington, DC 20044

Brigham Young University
Independent Study Course
236 Harman Building
P.O. Box 21514
Provo, UT 84602-1514
1-800-298-8792
http://coned.byu.edu/is/indstudy.htm

Council of Genealogy Columnists
c/o Regina Hines Ellison, CGRS
158 Lafayette Circle
Ocean Springs, MS 39564

Genealogical Institute of Mid-America
Continuing Education
Sangamon State University
Springfield, IL 62794-9243
217-786-7464

Institute on Genealogy and Historical Research
Samford University Library
Birmingham, AL 35229
205-870-2846
http://www.samford.edu/schools/ighr/ighr.html

National Genealogical Society
Education Department
4527 Seventeenth Street North
Arlington, VA 22207-2399

Repeat Performance
(Cassette tape recordings of genealogical lectures from
    conferences)
2911 Crabapple Lane
Hobart, IN 46342
219-465-1234

Salt Lake Institute of Genealogy
Utah Genealogical Association
P.O. Box 1144
Salt Lake City, UT 84110
888-463-6842

Periodical Publishers

Family Chronicle
10 Gateway Boulevard, Suite 490
P.O. Box 41301 STN BRM B
Toronto, ON M7Y 7E1
Canada

Everton's Genealogical Helper
The Everton Publishers
P.O. Box 368
Logan, UT 84323-0368

Heritage Quest Magazine
P.O. Box 329
Bountiful, UT 84011-0329

SELECTED READING

APG Directory of Professional Genealogists. Denver: Association of
Professional Genealogists, 1997.

Carmack, Sharon DeBartolo. *The Genealogy Sourcebook.* Los Angeles:
Lowell House (Chicago: Contemporary Books), 1997.

Clifford, Karen. *Becoming an Accredited Genealogist: Plus 100 Tips to
Ensure Your Success.* Salt Lake City: Ancestry, 1998.

Smith, Juliana Szucs. *The Ancestry Family Historian's Address Book: A
Comprehensive List of Local, State, and Federal Agencies and
Institutions and Ethnic and Genealogical Organizations.* Salt Lake
City: Ancestry, 1998.

Chapter Twelve

PRESERVING THE PAST FOR THE FUTURE

ORGANIZING YOUR FAMILY HISTORY

In a history seminar, the instructor asked each participant to write about the most important events that had occurred during his or her lifetime. To a person, all of the students wrote about events from personal life: marriage, their first children, school, etc. None wrote about the historical events of the time—the election of a president, the opening of Eastern Europe to democracy, new tax proposals. Obviously, the events of most importance to each person are personal experiences and relationships. Genealogy is the study of relationships— of ancestors who are directly related to us. They are our families; they are our role models. To learn more about them is to learn more about ourselves. How did they live? What trials did they endure? How did they overcome the difficulties in their lives? The answers to these questions lead us to investigate ever more our own family histories.

TRAFFORD COLE, PSY.D.
In *Italian Genealogical Records: How to Use Italian Civil, Ecclesiastical, and Other Records in Family History Research*

Every family historian has unique but always compelling reasons to keep family memories alive. We've been told that those who are remembered never die. Yet, our lives are increasingly crammed with activity; our jobs have splintered families, moving parts of them hundreds of miles from hometown roots; and television and other diversions occupy time that families used to spend in conversation.

Stories that had been handed down for generations in families are being lost. As memories fade, the intriguing accounts of the struggles and the accomplishments of our ancestors become shrouded in mystery. If we don't take steps to chronicle our own lives and preserve the histories of our families, they are in danger of being lost forever.

Previous chapters in this book highlighted fascinating records that can be used to find answers in solving family mysteries. This chapter is designed to help you organize the information and materials you collect and to preserve them as an heirloom from which future generations will benefit.

BEGINNING FAMILY HISTORY RESEARCH AND RECORD-KEEPING

A notebook and pencil get you started. That is one of the major appeals of genealogy—it requires only the basics, plus an inquiring mind and a sense of adventure. A tape recorder, though not essential, helps immeasurably to preserve the stories you hear. Someday those family members will be gone, and you will treasure the sound of their voices telling the tales of their past.

CHRISTINE ROSE, CG, CGL, AASG,
AND KAY GERMAIN INGALLS, CGRS
In *The Complete Idiot's Guide to Genealogy*

Begin by documenting your own life, then work backward through time and generations, taking one step at a time. Recording your own date and place of birth, your parents' names and birth dates, and other biographical information may seem simplistic, but it sets the foundation for building the family pedigree. Besides, once you're deeply absorbed in reconstructing the lives of other family members, it's easy to forget to record the events of your own life—the very information that future generations will want to know about you! Often you'll be surprised by what you find in these basic investigations. Misspelled names or inaccurate information recorded on your own birth certificate may be your first lesson on why "official" and other kinds of records are not entirely reliable. The names of forgotten or long-lost relatives may appear as witnesses to your parents' marriage, thus providing critical clues to further research. (It is not advisable to skip ahead several generations until you have solid proof for each person in your ancestral line.)

In her practical guide *Beyond Pedigrees: Organizing and Enhancing Your Work*, Beverly DeLong Whitaker suggests the following:

1. Organize, label, preserve, and present the mementos, photographs, and collections in your possession.
2. Write your own personal history.
3. Preserve an account of the early years of your children or your nieces and nephews.
4. Record the life histories of immediate ancestors whom you remember.
5. Gather details on more remote ancestors and create biographical sketches; annotate sources of information.

One of the most popular features of *Beyond Pedigrees* is that the author has set forth not only these and other basic steps for getting organized, but she has included some unusual charts that keep things straight and add fun to any project. Sections on "Organizing a Workspace" and "Documentation and Indexing Systems" are particularly helpful. Some of the more unusual charts and strategies that Whitaker illustrates and helps you create are:

Surname lists
Category lists
Census checklist
Checklist for evaluation
Correspondence list
Family history checklist
Ancestor checkpoints
Fact/opinion chart
Flowchart of research steps
Genealogical concept chart
Fan chart
Generation grid
Personal chronology
Place index
Tracings
Three-generation pedigree for correspondence
Personal Libraries and Archives Checklist

JOURNAL WRITING

Now in the 1990s, we find ourselves not only on the threshold of a new century, but the beginning of a new millennium. Aging baby boomers who wish to send a message into the future are largely responsible for a renewed interest in journals. People from a variety of professions such as psychologists, runners, clerics, and medical doctors are once again recognizing the many benefits to be obtained from keeping a journal.

JOAN NEUBAUER
In *Dear Diary: The Art and Craft of Writing a Creative Journal*

The history of journal writing goes back many centuries to some of the world's oldest civilizations. The Victorians of nineteenth-century England raised journal writing to a high art. Journals from the past give us rare and true insights into our own past. Over the last century, the popularity of journal-keeping has waned. In *Dear Diary: The Art and Craft of Writing a Creative Journal*, Joan Neubauer, known for her popular seminars on journal writing, shares her tips and experience for writing a creative journal. A companion to *Dear Diary* is *From Memories to Manuscript: The Five-Step Method of Writing Your Life Story*, in which Neubauer takes you through easy and enjoyable steps to creating your own autobiography as a work that others will want to read and preserve.

FAMILY HISTORY AND GENETICS

Typically, parents peer into a cradle and marvel at the perfection of the latest member of their family. Relatives arrive laden with gifts and the hope that the tiny miracle's life will be filled with health and happiness. The extended family also brings other intangible yet crucial legacies to the newborn. With each new wave of genetic research, it becomes increasingly apparent that a family passes on more than heirloom gifts to its new members.

> *Just as genes determine whether the baby's eyes will be blue or brown, they are also responsible for inherited family health factors which can influence the child's lifelong health. Knowing which of these diseases and disorders "run in the family" can help families make wise decisions about health and lifestyle and can assist health professionals in the earliest possible diagnosis of inherited medical problems.*
>
> LYNDA ANGELASTRO
> "Ancestors" (special edition of *Ancestry* magazine)

171

As you go back in time, charting your family's vital statistics and noting ages and causes of death, health patterns will emerge. Scientists have already identified several thousand hereditary diseases, and the list continues to grow. There are other medical disorders that, while not currently known to be inherited diseases, do tend to run in families. In studying the lifestyles of our ancestors, we find that daily habits and occupational hazards played a significant role in their longevity. Individual death certificates and the mortality schedules that were part of the federal census in some years reveal grim statistics that were a result of the widespread epidemics. Communicable diseases wiped out entire families and communities during our ancestors' lifetimes. Consciousness of many of the causes of premature deaths and a new appreciation for scientific advances are natural advantages that come with tracing your family history.

Many of these disorders and diseases were once considered incurable or life-threatening. Today, if they are diagnosed early enough, they can be successfully controlled or treated. And one of the most significant keys to early diagnosis and treatment is a comprehensive health history that can be accomplished as you research all the other aspects of family history.

Family health research should include the medical history not only of your direct ancestors but their brothers and sisters as well. It should include birth date; occupation; lifestyle information, such as drinking, smoking, or weight problems; significant medical conditions and the age at which they developed; known surgical procedures and the results; allergies; and the date and age at the time of the death. This information can be gleaned from your own memory; from medical records obtained from your family's doctor or hospital; from older relatives; or from obituaries in hometown newspapers. Add health information to pedigree charts and you will be providing each member of your family with a lifelong legacy of improved health.

How to Record

From the beginning of your family history project, make it a point to record all of your research activities. Cite the sources of all information as you gather it. Write down the source of every name, date, and place. Answer and record the following questions and analyze the reliability of each piece of information:

- Where did you find the name or date?

- Who recorded the information you are banking on to continue to research your family?

- Was the information you have collected for an individual found on a birth record, a death record, a census record, a cemetery record, or any other record entirely reliable?

- Is this piece of information from an undocumented family tradition? If so, be sure to make a record of it because it could be a valuable clue. However, be sure to note that it is only "tradition" until the story can be proved or disproved.

- Have birth dates and birthplaces been obtained from relatives or anyone else whose memory may not be entirely accurate? Note the circumstances of interviews.

- Was the information you have collected from a family history compiled by someone who was not careful in proving accuracy? Record the exact title of the family history, the author, and where you found the family history (name of library or individual who shared it with you).

PRESERVING YOUR HISTORICAL RECORDS AND MEMENTOS

Include the place that every piece of information was found and try to include at least a photocopied version of every record in your files. Some photographs, papers, and mementos that may come into your hands will be very unique and very fragile. At the onset, it is best to know how to preserve these historical items. For example, chemicals in pens and tapes and certain types of paper and plastic tend to ruin photographs, documents, and other materials with the passage of time.

In the process of research, we collect letters, newspaper clippings, legal documents, photocopies, computer printouts, books, photographs, photographic negatives, slides, old home movies, videotapes, sound recordings, computer disks, and textiles.

All of these items are subject to deterioration, which may occur chemically and/or physically. Chemical deterioration occurs when the chemical properties of an object react to heat or light. Brittleness in paper is a result of a chemical reaction within paper that was made using a sulfite pulping process.... Paper that has undergone chemical deterioration is weakened and can be easily damaged—even to the extent of crumbling in one's hand.

BARBARA SAGRAVES
In *A Preservation Guide: Saving the Past and Present for the Future*

A Preservation Guide provides information on cleaning, copying, encapsulating, deacidifying, and storing all the precious heirlooms mentioned above. It also includes an important chapter on "Disaster Recovery" that describes how to respond if your materials are damaged by storms, leaks, floods, insects, or fires. Sagraves also cautions, "Remember, if a document is truly unique, make a copy and store the original in a suitable archival box off-site."

SEARCH STRATEGY

It is generally more effective to concentrate on one family at a time, beginning with your immediate family.

- Define your search objectives and think about what records could give you information about these things.
- List the record sources you plan to search, where they are located, and think of how you can use them most effectively.
- Log results on the research calendar or correspondence chart as your research is completed.

GATHERING INFORMATION

If you're planning to interview someone, read up on how to conduct a good interview. There are a number of good books on the market that will get you off on the right track. "The Third Degree: Tips for a Successful Interview," by George

Thurston, *Ancestry* 16 (1), offers general guidelines that the author developed in forty-five years of observation and practice as a professional interviewer and journalist. Thurston suggests that knowing as much as possible about the person you will interview is the first rule of fruitful interviewing. "Give a lot of thought to the topics you want to cover" is another sound piece of advice given in the article. So that you don't forget to ask the most important questions of all, make a list of these in advance of the visit.

> *A systematic approach is critical to the success of any research trip. Without a rational, organized plan you will miss vital data, waste time, and overlook clues that you will not discover until you have returned home. When taking even a brief trip, a step-by-step approach—from the initial planning, through the trip itself, to the follow-up work when you return—will give you unexpected rewards in your research progress.*

> ANNE ROSS BALHUIZEN
> In *Searching on Location: Planning a Research Trip*

There is a certain value in approaching a research trip as a special activity. *Searching on Location* serves as a guide for the person who wants to make maximum use of his or her time, money, and energy in a specific quest for family history.

FILING AND ORGANIZING INFORMATION

Set up an organized filing system. You will be amazed at how quickly you accumulate documents and notes. Consider the fact that you have two parents, four grandparents, eight great-grandparents, sixteen great-great-grandparents, thirty-two great-great-great-grandparents, and so on. The average person has 1,024 direct-line ancestors within ten generations. Of course, you will be collecting information on all their siblings (collateral lines), and you will want to keep on file all the other

interesting things you run across
as you conduct your research.
Expect to amass a lot of paper! It
won't be a problem if you organize it well from the start.

As a rule, standard-size file
folders are the best way to organize and retrieve information. A
single file might contain all of
your findings on one surname for a time, but as the information accumulates, you'll probably find it necessary to break files
down by head of family (one generation), or by individuals. All
relevant documents and an inventory of what has been found
on each family or individual will then be at your fingertips
whenever needed.

Early in the research stage you will want to keep track of
what you have found in the specific geographic locations. For
example, if your ancestors lived in Brooklyn, New York, you
will need to learn as much as you can about the place before
you can effectively conduct research there. As you gather facts
about Brooklyn, you will want to photocopy pertinent information as it relates to your research there. A locality file is a good
place to keep a list of genealogical guides, local histories, lists of
records that have been microfilmed for the city, addresses and
telephone numbers, and any other sources that you will need to
refer to at later stages of your research. Likewise, it's a good idea
to keep other subject files.

If your ancestors were of German heritage, it will help to
keep a file on such things as a list of German genealogical
research guides, or German histories, or a clipping about
German immigration and passenger lists. All the subjects that
you are likely to use again are candidates for files. You'll be able
to readily retrieve your work if you organize it from the start.

NOTE-KEEPING

As you begin to gather information, it is extremely important to get into the habit of taking good notes. There are several organizing systems on the market, including computer software programs. Commercially produced computer programs have various methods of formatting and printing forms, but two standard genealogical forms discussed below will serve you whether you are using a computer or writing the data by hand onto preprinted forms.

ANCESTRAL/PEDIGREE CHART

The ancestral chart, or what is more often called a pedigree chart (figure 12-1), is a record of all the generational parents of a particular person. It shows, at a glance, the progress you have made and what remains to be found and proved. It is wise to keep two charts: (1) a work chart that records the names and minimum identifying information for each person assumed to be a direct ancestor; and (2) a permanent pedigree that records those ancestors who have been proved through careful research. Use a pencil on genealogical forms until you are confident about the data you have found. Most genealogical computer programs include special instructions on how to note proven information and distinguish it from undocumented sources.

The accepted style is to record males on the top half of the ancestral chart and the maternal lines on the bottom half. Pertinent information regarding their dates and places of birth, marriage, and death are recorded underneath. It is appropriate to indicate in some manner where the information was obtained.

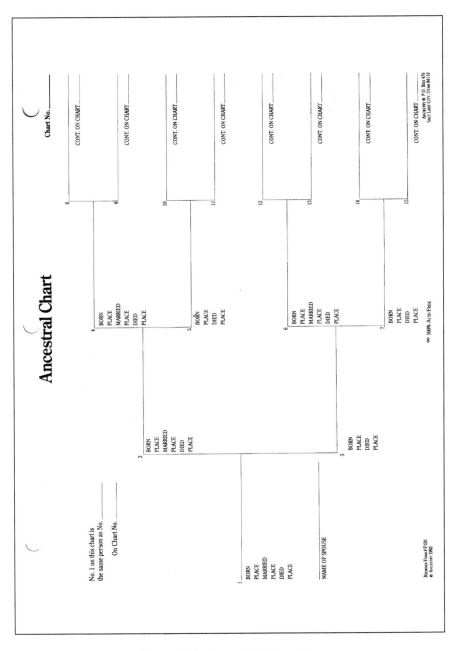

Figure 12-1. Ancestral/Pedigree Chart

To fill in an ancestral/pedigree chart:

- Place your name on line one, your father on line two, your mother on line three, and so on through the pedigree. Enter the names in the order in which they are written: given name, middle name, last name (maiden name if a woman). Printing surnames in all-uppercase letters (a standard practice) will help you to avoid confusion with names in which the surname is not immediately obvious, such as Dennis JAMES (James DENNIS); Kelly ARNOLD (Arnold KELLY); or May JOYCE (Joyce MAY) that could go either way.

- Enter the dates: day, month, year. Write the month or use standard abbreviations; never use a number to designate a month in genealogy. The European dating style is to enter the day/month/year, while Americans traditionally enter the month/day/year. Write all the numbers of the year; '98 could mean any century—is it 1898 or 1998?

- Enter the places: town or village, county or its equivalent, state or its equivalent. Items such as occupations, titles, places of residence, or changes of name can also be noted.
- Keep the worksheets in folders made for each surname.

Once careful research has proved the ancestors recorded on the work ancestral/pedigree chart to be correct, they may be entered in a similar way on your permanent charts.

FAMILY GROUP SHEETS

The family group sheet (figure 12-2) lists the immediate family of a particular couple (whether legally married or not), including their children, their parents, and other spouses. A typical group sheet has room for considerable data on each person (in order to trace collateral lines), and a reference for the source

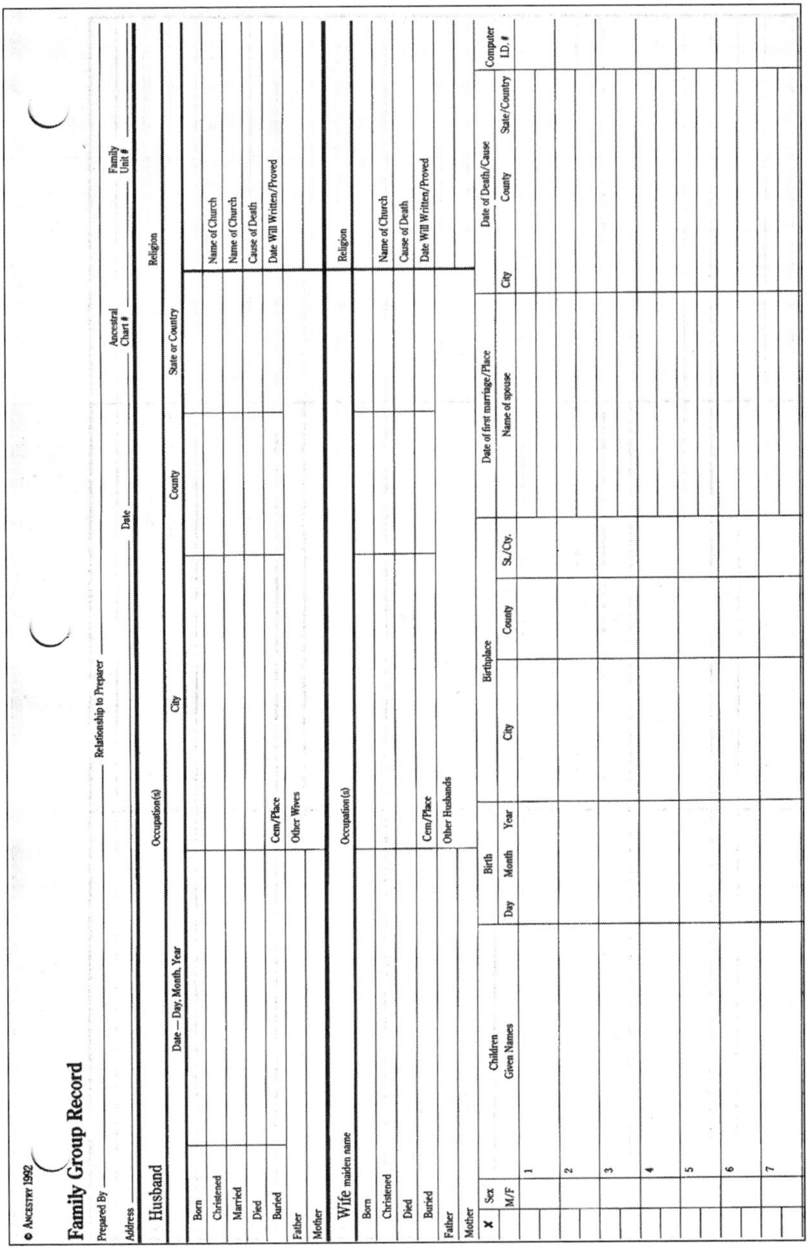

© ANCESTRY 1992

Family Group Record

Prepared By — Relationship to Preparer

Address — Date — Ancestral Chart # — Family Unit #

Husband — Occupation(s) — Religion

Date — Day, Month, Year | City | County | State or Country

Born
Christened — Name of Church
Married — Name of Church
Died — Cause of Death
Buried — Cem/Place — Date Will Written/Proved
Father — Other Wives
Mother

Wife maiden name — Occupation(s) — Religion

Born
Christened — Name of Church
Died — Cause of Death
Buried — Cem/Place — Date Will Written/Proved
Father — Other Husbands
Mother

✗	Sex M/F	Children Given Names	Birth Day	Birth Month	Birth Year	Birthplace City	Birthplace County	Birthplace St./Cty.	Date of first marriage/Place Name of spouse	Date of Death/Cause City	County	State/Country	Computer I.D. #
		1											
		2											
		3											
		4											
		5											
		6											
		7											

Figure 12-2. Family Group Sheet

of information. There should be a family group sheet for each couple on the ancestral chart and for each of their additional marriages. The final result of your research efforts will be to compile complete, correct, and connected families, and the use of family group sheets from the beginning will make the compilation much easier.

To fill in a family group sheet:

- Transcribe genealogical data from each source you search exactly as it appears—without changing the meaning or spelling—directly onto family group sheets. Note variations in spelling found in different record sources.

- Check your transcription against the source immediately to ensure that you've copied it accurately.

- Briefly describe the source from which the data was taken on the back of the family group sheet.

- Do not mix data. Record only one family on each sheet. If the family Bible gives information on five families, make out five family group sheets—one for each family.

- You may wish to note to the left of each parent's and child's name what information or proofs you already have for them (B = birth, M = marriage, D= death or burial, W = will, O = obituary, MIL = military, OTH = other information). You will then be able to see at a glance what records you have in your possession and what you still need to document.

RESEARCH CALENDARS

The research calendar gives you an account of every record source you have searched and serves as a reminder of what you have already done and where you have found pertinent information. Figure 12-3 is an example of how your research can be organized.

- Use a separate research calendar for each surname.

- Describe each search you make whether it yields information or not, and indicate the results of that search: no information located (nil) or see source summary (ss).

- List author, title, publisher, date and place of publication, name and address of repository or library where the record is located, and the call number, if it has one, for every record you consult.

- Note missing or torn pages, blurred entries, foreign languages, and indexes.

- Note personal visits while traveling. If you interview a relative, record the date of the interview and where the interview notes can be found.

CORRESPONDENCE LOG

It is important to keep track of those with whom you have corresponded, the reasons for writing, and whether or not you have received an answer in a correspondence log.

- Note each letter written, the address, the purpose, and the date the letter was sent, whether it was by mail, e-mail, fax, or personally delivered.

- As you receive answers to these letters, note the date and the information gleaned from them.

Family					
Researcher					
Date	Repository Call #/Microfilm #	Description of Source	Time Period/ Names Searched	Results	

Figure 12-3. Research Calendar

Source Summary for Family Information

Type of Information
B=Birth/Christening   F=Family (Children)
M=Marriage   A=Ancestral
D=Death/Burial   L=Land
W=Will   O=Obituary
MIL=Military   OTH=Other

Husband _____   Lineage Chart# _____

Wife _____   Individual # _____

Date	Repository Call #/Microfilm #	Name of Source Author/Publishing Date	Type of Info.	Information Found	File # (Optional)

Research Extract

File Number/Family	Repository	Call #/ Microfilm #

Description of Source _____

Indexed	Condition	Date

Time Period/Names Searched

Search Objective

Figures 12-4 and 12-5. Source Summary and Research Extract

SOURCE SUMMARY AND RESEARCH EXTRACT

It is helpful to be able to refer quickly to information you have found for a particular family and the sources of that information. Figures 12-4 and 12-5 illustrate the source summary and research extract.

- For each family group, keep a separate source summary of information found for that family group.

- Use research extract sheets to summarize information which cannot be photocopied, for which there is no document in your possession, or for things such as deeds which may be time consuming or difficult to reread quickly when you need information from the copy you have.

LOOSELEAF NOTEBOOKS

A looseleaf notebook can be divided into sections for ancestral charts, group sheets, vital research notes, correspondence, and other materials as you need them. If you carry the notebook with you while researching, you will have a quick reference to use for yourself and anyone from whom you seek help. When your family is charted, your line of research and thinking are much easier for another person to follow than your trying to describe the problem or remember everything yourself. As research continues and the files grow, you will probably want to have a notebook for each surname.

COMPUTER PROGRAMS

A number of wonderful genealogical computer programs are available to help you record, index, and preserve information, but it's not the intention of this guide to recommend one over another. Each program has its strengths and limitations. For up-to-date reviews of genealogical software, consult Eastman's Online Genealogy Newsletter or recent issues of *Genealogical Computing*.

Publishing and Sharing the Results of Your Research

As recently as two decades ago, genealogical publishing was accessible primarily to the affluent—and the process was overseen by genealogy and publishing professionals. In the 1990s word processors and laser printers put the power of publishing—information transfer—into the hands of most of us. With attention to standards we can produce professional-quality publications

Patricia Law Hatcher, CG
In *Producing a Quality Family History*

After all the time and effort that goes into research, who doesn't want the results of their work to be perpetuated? Pat Hatcher's acclaimed *Producing a Quality Family History* is a step-by-step guide that advises how to write a book that will be treasured for generations to come. Hatcher clearly details everything from typefaces and fonts, page layout and formatting (including photographs, charts, and illustrations), to organizing and presenting family information.

Lawrence P. Gouldrup, Ph.D.'s *Writing the Family Narrative* and *Writing the Family Narrative Workbook* will help you to enhance your writing style and turn your family history into an invaluable heirloom. In *Writing the Family Narrative,* Gouldrup skillfully shows how to produce a work in which seemingly disjointed facts can come together to entertain as well as to inform. His companion book, *Writing the Family Narrative Workbook*, takes you step-by-step through the writing process, providing plenty of room for collecting data, brainstorming, and trying new writing techniques. The workbook teaches you how to write with depth.

CONTRIBUTING YOUR FAMILY HISTORY
TO NATIONAL HISTORY

Not only do many researchers find connections with history through their genealogical investigations, but they also contribute both to the library and to future generations by publishing their findings in the form of family or regional histories. The library has become a major repository not only of individual family histories but also, in a larger sense, of the nation's memory as seen through the recounting of histories of local communities and families.

JAMES H. BILLINGTON
Former Librarian of Congress
In *The Library of Congress:
A Guide to Genealogical and Historical Research*

One of the great joys that comes with tracing a family history is sharing our research and discoveries with others. The Library of Congress actively seeks to acquire copies of every family history that is published. The gift of a book is not only a contribution to the library but to the global community.

Before you publish, or even if you never get to the stage of publishing your family history in book form, it is a wonderful idea to contribute your documented information to Ancestry's World Tree, the largest free database of family records online.

SELECTED READING

Balhuizen, Anne Ross. *Searching on Location: Planning a Research Trip.* Salt Lake City: Ancestry, 1992.

Cole, Trafford R. *Italian Genealogical Records: How to Use Italian Civil, Ecclesiastical, and Other Records in Family History Research.* Salt Lake City: Ancestry, 1995.

Gouldrup, Lawrence P. *Writing the Family Narrative.* Salt Lake City: Ancestry, 1987.

———. *Writing the Family Narrative Workbook.* Salt Lake City: Ancestry, 1993.

Hatcher, Patricia Law. *Producing a Quality Family History.* Salt Lake City: Ancestry, 1996.

Neagles, James C. *The Library of Congress: A Guide to Genealogical and Historical Research.* Salt Lake City: Ancestry, 1990.

Neubauer, Joan R. *Dear Diary: The Art and Craft of Writing a Creative Journal.* Salt Lake City: Ancestry, 1995.

———. *From Memories to Manuscript: The Five-Step Method of Writing Your Life Story.* Salt Lake City: Ancestry, 1994.

Rose, Christine, and Kay Germain Ingalls. *The Complete Idiot's Guide to Genealogy.* New York: Alpha Books, A Division of MacMillan Reference USA, 1997.

Sagraves, Barbara. *A Preservation Guide: Saving the Past and the Present for the Future.* Salt Lake City: Ancestry, 1995.

Whitaker, Beverly DeLong. *Beyond Pedigrees: Organizing and Enhancing Your Work.* Salt Lake City: Ancestry, 1993.

Appendix A

Sources of Family History Information

The following sources for tracing your family history are fully explained in *The Source: A Guidebook of American Genealogy*. Any of these information sources could provide valuable clues for tracing your family history.

Account books
Admiralty court records
Adoption records
Affidavits
Agricultural records
Alien registration records
Alimony records
Allotment records
Almshouse records
AMA Deceased Physician's File
Ancestral File™
Animal brands
Anniversary publications
Apprentice records

Archives
Army records
Assessment lists
Association records
Attorneys' records
Autobiographies
Bank records
Bankruptcy records
Bar Association records
Baronial records
Bible records
Bibliographies
Bills of sale
Biographical dictionaries and indexes
Birth data and birth records
Bishops' reports and transcripts
Bonds
Border crossing records
Boundary changes
Bounty-land grants
Bulletin boards (electronic)
Bureau of Indian Affairs
Bureau of Land Management
Bureau of Refugees, Freedmen, and Abandoned Lands
Burial grounds (family)
Burial records
Business and employment records
Business histories
Business incorporation records
Canal records
Cemetery records
Census records
Citizenship and naturalization records
Church records
City directories

City and town records
Civil War Records
Claims against the federal government
Clergy records
College records
Colonial records
Confederate records
Coroners' records
County histories
Court records
Credit reports
Criminal records
Customs records
DAR records
Death data and records
Deeds
Descriptive inventories
Diaries
Directories
Dispensation records
Divorce records
Draft records
Drivers' licenses
Electronic databases
Emigration records
Encyclopedias
Enlistment records
Enrollment records
Ethnic collections
Ethnic societies
Family group sheets
Family histories
LDS family history centers
LDS Family History Library
Family organizations

Maps
Marriage data and records
Medical records
Medical examiners' records
Membership records
Memorials
Merchant Marine records
Midwife records
Military records
Mortgage records
Motor vehicle records
Municipal archives
National Archives and Records Administration
National Personnel Records Center
Native American records
Naturalization records
Naval records
Newspapers
Obituaries
Occupational records
Online sources
Passenger lists
Passports
Patriotic societies
Pauper records
Pension records
Periodicals
Photographs
Pioneer histories and records
Port records
Probate records
Property records
Railroad records
School records
Social Security records

State archives
State historical societies
Tax records
Telephone books
Veterans' records
Vital records (birth, marriage, and death)
Yearbooks

$\mathcal{I}$NDEX

Work Projects Administration
(WPA)
naturalization indexes created by,
42
Soundex index system developed
by, 24
World Family Tree (online data-
base), 142, 189
World Wide Web, 128–50
WPA (Work Projects
Administration)
naturalization indexes created by,
42
Soundex index system developed
by, 24
Writing the Family Narrative
(Gouldrup), 188

Y
Yahoo! (search engine), 129
Yearbooks, at historical societies, 78

Z
Zero, in Soundex surname codes,
25

 $\mathcal{L}$ORETTO KATHRYN DENNIS SZUCS— "Lou"—holds a B.A. degree in history from Saint Joseph's College in Indiana and has been involved in genealogical research, teaching, lecturing, and publishing for more than twenty-five years.

Lou is the author of several publications, including *They Became Americans: Finding Naturalizations Records and Ethnic Origins* and *Chicago and Cook County Sources: A Genealogical and Historical Guide*. With Sandra Luebking, she co-authored *The Archives: A Guide to the National Archives Field Branches*. She and Sandra are also co-editors of *The Source: A Guidebook of American Genealogy* (rev. ed.).